# The First Gay Pope

## and other records

by

**Lynne Yamaguchi Fletcher**

Boston ♦ Alyson Publications, Inc.

Typeset and printed in the United States of America.

This is a paperback original from Alyson Publications, Inc.,
40 Plympton St., Boston, Mass. 02118.
Distributed in England by GMP Publishers,
P.O. Box 247, London N17 9QR, England.

This book is printed on acid-free, recycled paper.

First edition, first printing: December 1992

5  4  3  2  1

ISBN 1-55583-206-7

# THE FIRST GAY POPE

# CONTENTS

Introduction : 7

History : 9

Language : 22

Theory : 25

Community : 29

Education : 51

Religion : 57

Politics : 63

Law : 75

The arts : 85

Visual : 87

Literature : 87

Theatre : 97

Film : 101

Music : 102

The media : 107

Print : 109

Radio : 116

Television : 117

*Coax me, wild geese,*
*with your steadfast flight,*
*back to that estuarine shore.*

# INTRODUCTION

Welcome to the first compilation of gay and lesbian firsts and records. Be forewarned: this is not the definitive edition — yet. The information contained here is wide-ranging and as accurate as possible given the time and resources I had, but many holes remain, holes that I hope readers will help me fill. Some entries are speculative, as I've tried to indicate with more-tentative wording. Some are obviously incomplete, missing names or precise dates or other facts; what's stated is what I know. And so new are we to noting our history that even items accepted as fact are not cast in stone. If you notice an error or can supply missing details, please let me know. If you know something that belongs here, drop me a letter, with as many details as you can provide. This is an opportunity for us as a community to take note of our achievements, and to mark the milestones that let us see how we came to be.

Note, too, that though the book aims at an international scope, some areas — politics and the media, for example — are decidedly American. Here especially, contributions are needed to supplement the limited resources available in English.

Thanks are due many for enabling this work to exist. Historians and activists and keepers of mementoes — you who remember enable all of us to keep moving forward. I am particularly indebted to Garland Press's *Encyclopedia of Homosexuality,* edited by Wayne Dynes; the *Advocate,* for twenty-five years of record keeping; Stephen Donaldson; *The Alyson Almanac;* Leigh Rutledge's *Gay Decades* and *Gay Book of Lists;* Jonathan Katz's

*Gay/Lesbian Almanac* and *Gay American History;* Kay Tobin and Randy Wicker's *Gay Crusaders;* Toby Marotta's *Politics of Homosexuality;* Del Martin and Phyllis Lyon's *Lesbian/Woman;* Kaier Curtin's *We Can Always Call Them Bulgarians;* Dell Richards's *Lesbian Lists;* Stuart Timmons's *The Trouble with Harry Hay;* Marie Kuda; Paul Hennefeld; William Edward Glover; Carol Seajay; Eric Garber; countless other large and small publications; and the many people who sent in individual contributions. Thanks go, too, to my friend and colleague Karen Barber, for help in tracking down those final loose ends, and to the rest of the Alyson staff, for their daily support. And finally, for abiding with me through thick and thicker, I thank my ever-loving partner, Cate.

*Lynne Yamaguchi Fletcher*

# HISTORY

### advice on cruising, the first published
*The Art of Love,* by the Roman poet Publius Ovid, circa
A.D. 1. His favorite cruising spots were the market, the temple,
and the racetrack. He cruised both men and women, and included in his poem advice to women seeking men.

### advocate, the first homosexual rights
Heinrich Hoessli (1784–1864). His two-volume *Eros: Die
Männerliebe der Griechen* [*Eros: The Male Love of the Greeks*],
published in 1836–1838, protested society's intolerance of
homosexuality and argued the naturalness of homosexual
love. Though it was read by only a small audience in his
lifetime, it was a harbinger of the homosexual rights movement that would arise at the end of the century.

### celebrity, the first out in modern times
André Gide. He made public his homosexuality in his 1926
autobiography, *Si le grain ne meurt* [*If It Die*].

### cemetery, the world's gayest
Père-Lachaise, in Paris. Among the notable gays and bisexuals
buried here are Gertrude Stein, Alice B. Toklas, Oscar Wilde,
Isadora Duncan, Jane Avril, Sarah Bernhardt, Marcel Proust,
Rosa Bonheur, Natalie Micus, Anna Klümpke (these three
buried together in the Micus family plot!), Colette, and the
"French Sappho" Anna de Noailles. Also buried here in one of
the most talked-about monuments in the cemetery are two
nineteenth-century balloonists, Croce-Spinelli and Sivel, who
died together in a ballooning accident in India in 1875. The
marble monument over the tomb they share shows the two
lying together naked, hand-in-hand and holding flowers,
under a sculpted sheet that covers them from the waist down.

**city, the first to be founded in honor of a gay lover**
Antinoopolis, founded in Egypt by the Roman emperor
Hadrian (ca. 111–130) in the second century, after his lover
Antinous drowned.

**city, the gayest, in number of bars and cafes**
Berlin. In 1932, the German city had some 300 gay bars and
cafes, with a tenth geared toward lesbians.

**conviction, the first known in North America for lesbian
activity**
Sarah White Norman. In March 1649, she and Mary Vincent
Hammon, both married, were charged with "lewd behavior
each with [the] other upon a bed" in Plymouth, Massachusetts.
The charges against Hammon were dropped, perhaps because
of her young age (she was fifteen), but Norman was convicted
and had to publicly confess her "unchaste behavior."

**conviction, the first known in North America for sodomy**
Richard Cornish of the Virginia Colony. He was tried and,
despite flimsy evidence, hanged for sodomy in 1624.

**couple, the first documented gay**
Pharoah Phiops II of Egypt (2355–2261 B.C.) and his general
Sisinne.

**cross-dresser, the first known female**
The Egyptian queen Hatshepsut, who reigned from 1503 to
1482 B.C. Wearing male attire and a fake beard that signified
kingship, she ruled Egypt as pharaoh for nearly twenty years
after her husband's death.

**dictionary, the first English-language of sexual information**
*The Encyclopedia of Sexual Knowledge,* edited by the
Australian homophile Norman Haire in 1934.

**execution, the last for homosexuality in Britain**
1836. The death penalty for sodomy would remain on the
books until 1861, however.

**gift, the greatest to a same-sex lover**
The Chinese empire. During his reign, Emperor Ai (r. 6 B.C.–
A.D. 1), the last adult emperor of the Han dynasty, rewarded
his beloved, Dong Xian, with a large fortune and a series of
high offices. And on his deathbed, over his councillors' objec-
tions, Ai gave Dong Xian the imperial seals, intending for him
to succeed him. Lacking sufficient support, Dong Xian was
soon forced to kill himself, and the Han dynasty was left to be
overthrown.

**graffiti, the oldest known gay**
On the Greek island of Santorin, formerly Thera. The inscrip-
tions date from the sixth century B.C., and appear to record
homosexual acts performed as rites of initiation.

**grave, the first joint homosexual**
The Tomb of the Two Brothers, at Thebes. This Egyptian sepul-
cher from the third millenium B.C. contains the remains of two
men believed to be lovers, Niankhnum and Khnumhotep. Bas
reliefs on the walls show the two embracing.

### history, the first comprehensive of homosexuality

*Duan xiu pian* [*Records of the Cut Sleeve*], compiled anonymously during China's Ming dynasty (1368–1644). Collected here are descriptions of homosexual encounters from 2,000 years' worth of sources. This first history of Chinese homosexuality is most likely the first comprehensive history of homosexuality anywhere in the world.

### holiday, the first gay

Robigalia, celebrated April 25 in ancient Rome. The holiday was dedicated to male prostitutes.

### homosexual, candidates for the first

The serpent in Genesis. According to Gnostic thinking, as recorded in Hippolytus's account of the Naassenes in *Refutation of All Heresies,* the serpent had homosexual intercourse with Adam, and introduced depravity to the world.

Orpheus. After his wife Eurydice's death, Orpheus was said to have turned to young men for comfort.

King Laius. According to some Greek sources, the man who would later father Oedipus was banished from Thebes and sought refuge at the court of Pelops. Falling in love with Pelops's beautiful twelve-year-old son, Chrysippus, Laius kidnapped and raped him. Chysippus killed himself, and Pelops pronounced the curse that would be Laius's undoing: that Laius would have a son who would "kill his father, marry his mother, and bring ruin on his native city."

Lot. Though in the Hebrew Bible, God favors Lot by warning him to flee Sodom before its destruction, Arabs appear to hold him responsible for the "sin of Sodom," calling homosexuals "the people of Lot."

**homosexual, the first self-identified to publicly call for an
end to persecution**

Karl Heinrich Ulrichs, on August 29, 1867. Addressing a conference of 500 jurists in Munich, Ulrichs courageously spoke
out against the persecution of homosexuals. No gay person
had ever spoken out in person on the subject of homosexuality before.

**images, the oldest surviving explicitly homosexual**

Greek vase paintings. Sexually explicit paintings that depict
an older man having intercrural or anal intercourse with a
younger one have been found on ceramic vases dating back
to the early sixth century B.C. In addition, a fresco on one wall
of the Etruscan Tomb of the Bulls in Tarquinia, Italy, dated at
around 540 B.C., shows a man anally penetrating another who
has horns and is being charged by a bull.

**institutionalization, the first of pederasty**

On Crete, in the Minoan (3000–1000 B.C.) or Archaic period
(800–500 B.C.), perhaps as a means of population control.

**king, the first homosexual**

Phiops II (a.k.a. Pepy II Neferkare; 2355–2261 B.C.). The last
great pharaoh of Egypt is said to have had an affair with his
general Sisinne. The pair was the first historically documented
gay couple.

**lambda symbol, the first use of the**

In 1969, by the Gay Activists Alliance in New York City. The
group, which formed in the wake of the Stonewall riots,
adopted the Greek letter as its symbol at the suggestion of
member Tom Doerr, based on its scientific use as a symbol of
kinetic potential in physics.

**law, the first to prescribe the death penalty for sodomy**
The Holiness Code of Leviticus, adopted by Darius I in the
fifth century B.C. Leviticus 20:13 specifies: "If a man also lie
with mankind, as he lieth with a woman, both of them have
committed an abomination: they shall surely be put to death;
their blood shall be upon them."

**list, the first of notable homosexuals of the past**
The first serious attempt at such a list appeared in the second
volume of *Eros: Die Männerliebe der Griechen* [*Eros: The Male
Love of the Greeks*], by Heinrich Hoessli, published in 1838.
The most notable effort previous to that appeared in Voltaire's
1764 *Dictionnaire philosophique,* under the article "L'Amour
nommé Socratique."

**memorial, the first dedicated to gay Holocaust victims**
A pink granite stone monument at the site of the Neuen-
gamme Nazi concentration camp in Germany. Unveiled May
12, 1985, and bearing the inscription "Dedicated to the Homosexual victims of National Socialism, 1985," the monument was
erected by Independent Alternative Homosexuals, a gay organization in Hamburg.

**memorial, the first gay and lesbian**
The Stichting Homo-Monument in Amsterdam, dedicated in
1987. This public sculpture "commemorates all women and
men who were ever oppressed and persecuted because of
their homosexuality." Designed by Karin Daan, the sculpture
consists of a giant pink granite triangle, 107 feet on each side,
containing three smaller triangles. One points to the Anne
Frank House; one points to the headquarters of the COC, the
Dutch gay rights organization; the third extends like a wharf
into the Keizersgracht canal.

### military unit, the first gay

The Sacred Band of Thebes, formed circa 371 B.C. This small army, made up of 150 male couples, was premised on the belief that lovers fighting alongside each other would die together rather than shame each other. The band perished to the last man at Chaeronea in 338 B.C., in battle against the huge army of Philip of Macedon.

### organization, the world's first homosexual rights

The Scientific-Humanitarian Committee (Wissenschaftlich-humanitäre Komitee), founded in Berlin by Magnus Hirschfeld, a Jewish physician who became the world's leading authority on homosexuality, on May 14, 1897, his twenty-ninth birthday. Its goal was legal tolerance and social acceptance for homosexuals. The Committee's activities included fighting, albeit unsuccessfully, for the repeal of the anti-homosexual Paragraph 175 of the German penal code; educating the public; publishing the world's first scholarly journal on homosexuality; and coordinating the study of all aspects of homosexuality. The organization lasted thirty-six years, ending with Hitler's rise to power.

### outing, the first case of

Adolf Brand (1874–1745) outed the imperial chancellor of Germany in 1907. Brand, the editor of the homosexual periodical *Der Eigene,* was working to repeal the anti-homosexual Paragraph 175 of the German penal code when the Eulenburg scandal broke in 1906. (Eulenburg was a German diplomat whose homosexual involvements had led to a security breach during the Morocco crisis of 1906. Because of his closeness to Kaiser Wilhelm II, the exposure of his homosexuality sent shock waves throughout the republic.) Learning that the chancellor, Bernhard Prince von Bülow, a member of Eulenburg's circle, was romantically involved with his secretary, Brand wrote and distributed a leaflet exposing Bülow as a homosexual. Bülow sued for libel. Because of the political climate,

Brand was railroaded — convicted and sentenced to eighteen months in prison. Brand's motivation in exposing Bülow foreshadowed the current justifications given for outing. In Brand's own words: "When someone — as teacher, priest, representative, or statesman — would like to set in the most damaging way the intimate love contact of others ... in that moment his own love life ceases to be a private matter."

### pink triangle, the first use of the

1937. Prisoners in Nazi concentration camps had to wear triangular patches identifying their status: green for criminals, red for Communists, blue for illegal emigrés, black for "asocials" (some believe this included lesbians), purple for Jehovah's Witnesses, brown for Gypsies, yellow for Jews, and pink for homosexuals. In the hierarchy that developed within the camps, inmates wearing pink triangles — estimated to number in the tens of thousands — were among those at the bottom. As a result, homosexuals suffered an extremely high death rate. Many were worked to death, died the targets of brutality or the subjects of "medical experiments," or starved on a diet intentionally below the minimum needed for survival. In the 1970s, gay activists discovered the pink triangle's history and adopted it as a symbol of resistance and solidarity.

### political party, the first to support gay rights

The German Social Democratic party. This was the only party to support the demands of the Scientific-Humanitarian Committee when it submitted its first petition for repeal of the antihomosexual Paragraph 175 of the German penal code in January 1898.

**pope, the first gay**
Benedict IX (ca. 1020–1055). An earlier pope, John XII (937–964), might also be a contender for this title; his enthusiastic bisexuality was widely known. But John XII, who died in bed with a woman, was best known for his heterosexual excesses. Benedict, who turned the Vatican into a male brothel, was the first pope known to be primarily homosexual.

**prostitute, the first documented homosexual male**
Timarchus of Athens (ca. 346 B.C.). Timarchus was certainly not the first homosexual prostitute, but his case is documented because he was a free citizen accused of prostituting himself to sailors. The accusation was politically motivated; found guilty, Timarchus lost his right as a free citizen to speak before the Athenian assembly.

**public figure, the first in the U.S. to publicly support gay rights**
Emma Goldman (1869–1940). A firm supporter of Wilde during his prosecution, Goldman began speaking publicly on the issue of homosexuality in 1910.

**saint, the first rumored to be gay**
St. John the Evangelist. He is traditionally identified as the unnamed disciple "whom Jesus loved," and who lay on Christ's bosom at the Last Supper (John 13:23). Medieval devotional images of John with his head in Christ's lap gave rise to mystical texts in which John is said to have enjoyed "the milk of the Lord." Not until the sixteenth century, however, did anyone explicitly assert a sexual relationship between Jesus and John; the claim remains doubtful at best.

**scholar, the first gay**

Heinrich Hoessli (1784–1864). In 1836–1838, this Swiss-German milliner wrote and published himself what could be called the first comprehensive study of homosexuality, a two-volume plea for social tolerance called *Eros: Die Männerliebe der Griechen: Ihre Beziehungen zur Geschichte, Erziehung, Literature, und Gesetzgebung aller Zeiten* [*Eros: The Male Love of the Greeks: Its Relationship to the History, Education, Literature, and Legislation of All Ages*].

**separatist community, the first known women-only in the U.S.**

The Sanctificationists commune in Belton, Texas, founded in 1866 by Martha McWhirter (?–1904). This semi-religious group consisted mostly of married women who left their marriages to join the commune, drawing disapproval from the community. The commune flourished, however. After their home became overcrowded, the women built a hotel, which became their main financial support. The women were self-sufficient; educated themselves; had their own dentist, shoemaker, and so forth; and traveled in small groups. In 1899, when their Texas site became too small for their increasing numbers, they moved to Washington, D.C.

**sex-change operation, the first in the U.S.**

The first complete sex-change operation in the U.S. was performed in 1968 by Dr. John Money of Johns Hopkins University.

**sex-change operation, the first known female-to-male**

Michael Dillon's, completed in 1949 in London after a series of thirteen phalloplastic operations performed over a four-year period.

**sex-change operation, the first well-known male-to-female**
Christine Jorgensen's, performed in Copenhagen, Denmark, in 1952, by a Danish plastic surgeon, Paul Fogh-Andersen. Once a sergeant in the American army, Jorgensen died in 1989 after living almost forty years as a woman. Hers was the first publicized sex change, though the first modern, medically supervised sex change on record was performed in Europe in 1930.

**spy, the first known homosexual**
Raymond Lecomte (1857–1921). As the first secretary of the French legation in Berlin, Lecomte infiltrated the homosexual clique surrounding the German Prince Philipp von Eulenburg. His discovery that Germany was bluffing in the Morocco crisis of 1906 led to a French diplomatic victory at the Algeciras Conference. This in turn led to Eulenburg's exposure as a homosexual and his subsequent ruin. Lecomte's activities are the first known instance of a homosexual's using his sexual contacts for espionage.

**suicide, the first known to be related to homosexuality**
Heinrich von Kleist's, in 1811. This German playwright and short story writer killed himself at the age of thirty-four in a joint pact made with a terminally ill female friend.

**transsexual, the first known**
The Roman emperor Heliogabalus (204–222). This highly effeminate ruler offered a large reward to any physician who could give him female genitalia. No one could.

### U.S. president, the first rumored to have loved men

George Washington (1732–1799). Though married, Washington surrounded himself with a "family" of male intimates, including his aide Alexander Hamilton, whose affection for John Laurens is well documented. Also rumored to be gay was James Buchanan (1791–1868), the unmarried fifteenth president of the United States. Buchanan's close friend Senator William King, known around Washington as "Miss Nancy," was branded "Buchanan's better half" by Andrew Johnson.

# LANGUAGE

### AIDS, the first use of the label

The Acquired Immune Deficiency Syndrome label was coined at a Centers for Disease Control (CDC) meeting held July 27, 1982, in Washington, D.C., with representatives from the blood industry, hemophiliac groups, gay community organizations, the National Institute of Health, and the Food and Drug Administration. The disease had first been called "gay cancer" because of the prominence of Kaposi's sarcoma as a symptom. Among the early proposed acronyms were GRID (Gay-Related Immune Deficiency), ACIDS (Acquired Community Immune Deficiency Syndrome), and CAIDS (Community Acquired Immune Deficiency Syndrome).

### *bisexual*, the first recorded use of the word

In its current sense, in 1892, in Charles Gilbert Chaddock's translation of Krafft-Ebing's *Psychopathia Sexualis*. The word's original meaning was "having the sexual organs of both sexes," used from the 1810s in reference to plants.

***faggot,* the first recorded use of the word in reference to homosexuals**

In a vocabulary of criminal slang published in Portland, Oregon, in 1914. "All the fagots (sissies) will be dressed in drag at the ball tonight," read the usage example. The shortened form *fag* first appeared in print nine years later in *The Hobo,* by Nels Anderson (1923): "Fairies or Fags are men or boys who exploit sex for profit."

***gay,* the first recorded use of the word in reference to homosexuality**

In the American *Underworld and Prison Slang,* by Noel Ersine, published in 1935. The entry was for *geycat,* "a homosexual boy." Though this was the first unambiguous use of the word in print in a homosexual context, it was in spoken use for more than a decade before. Indeed, in 1922, Gertrude Stein published a short story called "Miss Furr and Miss Skeene," in which two women live together learning "ways of being gay." "She was gay enough," Miss Furr finds, "she was always gay exactly the same way, she was always learning little things to use in being gay ... she would always be gay in the same way..."

***homophobia,* the first recorded use of the word**

In a 1967 book, *Homosexual Behavior among Males,* by Wainwright Churchill.

### *homosexuality,* the first recorded use of the word

May 6, 1868, in a draft of a private letter from Károly Mária Kertbeny (Karl Maria Benkert, 1824–1882) to Karl Heinrich Ulrichs. The first public use of the term was in a pamphlet published anonymously in early 1869 by Kertbeny urging the repeal of anti-gay laws. The pamphlet, the first of two that Kertbeny published that year, was titled *143 des Preussischen Strafgesetzbuchs und seine Aufrechterhaltung als 152 des Entwurfs eines Strafgesetzbuchs für den Norddeutschen Bund* [*Paragraph 143 of the Prussian Penal Code and Its Maintenance as Paragraph 152 of the Draft of a Penal Code for the North German Confederation*]. In it, Kertbeny used the word *Homosexualität* [homosexuality] instead of Ulrichs's term *Urningtum, Homosexualisten* [homosexual] instead of *Urninge,* and *Homosexualistinnen* [lesbian] instead of *Urninden.* Though one of the most important of the early gay rights activists, Kertbeny himself claimed to be a *Normalsexualer,* not a homosexual.

The term came into common use after being popularized by the press during the scandalous Harden-Eulenburg affair that erupted in late 1906.

The *Oxford English Dictionary* credits the first use of the term in English to Charles Gilbert Chaddock, who in his 1892 translation of Krafft-Ebing's *Psychopathia Sexualis* rendered the German cognate as "homo-sexuality."

### *lesbianism,* the first recorded use of the word

In a May 2, 1870, diary entry by A.J. Munby, who wrote, "Swinburne ... expressed ... an actual admiration of Lesbianism..."

### slang term, the oldest known English for a homosexual man

*Molly.* The use of this woman's name as a label for effeminate homosexuals originated with "molly houses," male brothels, in early eighteenth-century London. Raids on these brothels in 1699, 1707, and 1727 led to their notoriety. The term *molly house* itself may originate with the woman's name, a diminutive of Mary; with the Latin *mollis,* "soft, effeminate"; or with some fusion of the two.

### slang term, the oldest known English for a lesbian

*Bull-dyker, bull-dyke,* or *bull-dyking* (also *B.D.*) *woman.* American blacks appear to have coined these terms in the 1920s. *Dyke* most likely comes from *dike,* a late nineteenth-century slang term meaning "to dress up formally or elegantly."

# THEORY

### book, the first English-language to treat homosexuality neutrally

*Sexual Inversion,* by Havelock Ellis, published in November 1897. In this book, first published in 1896 in German as *Das konträre Geschlectsgefühl* [*Contrary Sexual Feeling*], with John Addington Symonds as coauthor, Ellis treated homosexuality as neither a crime nor a disease, and urged public toleration of what he considered an inborn condition. The English publisher was prosecuted for obscenity. The book was later reissued as the second volume of Ellis's seven-volume *Studies in the Psychology of Sex.*

**paper, the first modern medical to focus on homosexuality**
An article by the German Karl Friedrich Otto Westphal (1833–1890) published in 1869 in *Archiv für Psychiatrie und Nervenkrankheiten*. In it he described two cases he was observing, one of a lesbian, the other of a male transvestite, labeling his subjects' condition *die contraire Sexualempfindung,* contrary sexual feeling.

**paper, the first modern medical to mention homosexuality**
An 1833 paper by anatomist Robert Froriep. In a note appended to the paper, Johann Ludwig Casper (1796–1864), an expert in forensic medicine, mentioned observing an accused pederast who showed no desire for the opposite sex.

**paper, the first psychiatric to mention homosexuality**
Written in 1849 by Claude-François Michéa (1815–1882). Studying the case of a necrophiliac, Michéa theorized the existence of a whole series of "erotic mono-manias," including attraction to members of one's own sex, citing Sappho as an example of the latter. Michéa's isolated study had no impact on medical thinking at the time.

**paper, the first scientific on homosexuality**
A case history of two men who loved members of their own sex, published in 1791 in the *Magazine of Experimental Psychical Studies,* a German scientific journal.

### psychiatrist, the first to realize that homosexuality was more than an individual phenomenon

Vladimir Fiodorovich Chizh (1855–19??). This Russian psychiatrist was the first to realize, in 1882, that homosexuality was a general condition, not merely a phenomenon of isolated cases, that could be used to explain many of the sodomy cases appearing in the courts of the day.

### study, the first to show homosexuals are not mentally ill

Evelyn Hooker's 1957 "The Adjustment of the Male Overt Homosexual." Until the 1950s, clinical studies of homosexuals were based on observations of mental patients or prisoners. In the mid-1950s, however, working at the University of California at Los Angeles, Hooker set out to study the adjustment of a randomly selected sample of homosexual men taken from the larger community. It took her two years to find enough willing subjects. In the end, she compared a group of thirty individuals with a control group of thirty heterosexual men, paired for age, education, and I.Q. Each subject underwent a battery of three commonly used projective personality tests. Three independent experts then evaluated the data obtained for each subject. Finding no single pattern of homosexual adjustment, Hooker concluded that:

1. Homosexuality as a clinical entity does not exist. Its forms are as varied as those of heterosexuality.

2. Homosexuality may be a deviation in sexual pattern which is within the normal range psychologically...

3. The role of particular forms of sexual desire and expression in personality structure may be less important than has been frequently assumed. Even if one assumes that homosexuality represents a severe form of maladjustment to society in the sexual sector of behavior, this does not necessarily mean that the homosexual must be severely maladjusted in other sectors of his behavior...

**theorist, the first to conceptualize homosexuals as a minority**

Kurt Hiller (1885–1972), in 1921. A German leftist and homosexual rights activist, Hiller said in a September 21 address that "human beings are marked not only by differences of race and character type, but also of ... sexual orientation." This concept took on new life in August 1944, when Robert Duncan (1919–1988), the American poet, published his essay "The Homosexual in Society," in the anarchist magazine *Politics,* arguing that homosexuals, like Jews and blacks, are an oppressed minority.

**theorist, the first to distinguish between innate and acquired homosexuality**

Aristotle (384–322 B.C.), in his *Nicomachean Ethics.*

**theory, the first medical of homosexuality**

Presented in the Greek *Hippocratic Corpus,* a collection of medical treatises written by a school of physicians from the sixth to the first century B.C. According to the theory, both parents secrete male or female "bodies." If the father's secretion was female, rather than male, and the mother's was male, the result would be either a "man-woman" — an effeminate male — or a "mannish" female.

# COMMUNITY

### AIDS-related death, the first documented of a gay man

Occurred in January 1979 in Cologne, Germany. A 42-year-old German concert violinist died after battling Kaposi's sarcoma, a lymph infection, and a series of mysterious diseases.

### archive, the first and largest lesbian

The Lesbian Herstory Archives in New York. Founded by Joan Nestle and Deborah Edel in 1974, its collection now includes more than 6,000 books, 13,000 periodical titles, 500 unpublished papers, and 12,000 photographs, films, and oral histories. Having outgrown its original home in the apartment of cofounder Nestle, the archive recently moved to its own four-story building in Brooklyn.

### archive, the largest gay and lesbian in the U.S.

The International Gay and Lesbian Archive in Los Angeles. The IGLA contains some 25,000 books related to homosexuality, as well as clippings, photographs, works of art, and memorabilia. Begun as a private collection by curator Jim Kepner in 1943, it opened as a public institution in Hollywood in 1979.

### athlete, the first professional to come out as gay

David Kopay, in 1975. A pro running back for ten years, Kopay played for the San Francisco Forty-Niners, the Detroit Lions, the Washington Redskins, the New Orleans Saints, and the Green Bay Packers. He came out in an interview by reporter Lynn Rosellini in the *Washington Star* in December 1975, the first pro athlete in any sport to voluntarily admit his homosexuality.

### business association, the first gay

The Tavern Guild, an organization of gay-bar owners, founded in San Francisco in 1962.

### cause célèbre, the first gay

The Dale Jennings entrapment case in 1952. Jennings was falsely arrested in Los Angeles for solicitation. Instead of shamefully accepting his victimization, as most homosexuals did at the time, Jennings, a member of the newly formed Mattachine Society, decided to fight. The Mattachine Foundation formed an independent Citizen's Committee to Outlaw Entrapment and waged a public campaign to fight the practice. When the case went to trial on June 23, 1952, Jennings made history by openly admitting his homosexuality, defending himself instead by accusing the arresting officer of entrapment. The case was dismissed after the jury deadlocked. This can be called the first activist action in the modern American gay liberation movement.

### coalition, the first national of gay rights groups

The National Planning Conference of Homophile Organizations, established at a Kansas City conference attended by fifteen groups in February 1966. The next year it adopted a more formal structure and changed its name to the North American Conference of Homophile Organizations (NACHO). Until it broke up in August 1970, NACHO provided an important forum for creating a national gay rights movement, comprising fifty member organizations by 1969. Among its accomplishments were a national legal fund, nationally coordinated public demonstrations, and a number of regional projects.

### coalition, the first of gay rights organizations

East Coast Homophile Organizations (ECHO), founded in Philadelphia in January 1963. Frank Kameny initiated the effort; four organizations joined: the Washington and New York chapters of the Mattachine Society, the New York chapter of Daughters of Bilitis, and the Janus Society of Philadelphia. ECHO was later succeeded by the larger, more ambitious Eastern Regional Conference of Homophile Organizations (ERCHO).

### community center, the first gay in North America

The SIR Center, founded by the Society for Individual Rights in San Francisco in April 1966.

### conference, the first national lesbian

The first national Daughters of Bilitis convention, held in San Francisco in May 1960.

### couple, the first lesbian to dance at the White House

Barbara Love of New York and Kay Whitlock of Philadelphia waltzed to chamber music in the outer lobby in 1978 after going to the White House with an International Women's Year committee to present the IWY National Plan of Action to President Carter.

### couple, the first openly lesbian to join the National Organization for Women

Del Martin and Phyllis Lyon, in 1968. They joined NOW's San Francisco chapter, applying for and receiving a reduced rate for membership as a couple.

**couple, the first same-sex to be featured in *People* magazine's "Couples" section**
Dr. Tom Waddell and Charles Deaton, in 1987.

**credit card, the first gay**
Issued by the Pride Foundation of Seattle through Seafirst National Bank. First issued in December 1990, the card is available only in the five northwest states. A portion of every purchase and of the $18 annual fee goes to the Pride Foundation, which disperses it to other nonprofit, gay and lesbian, women's rights, and AIDS support groups. A second card, issued by the Dallas Gay Alliance Credit Union, is the first to feature the word *gay* on it. Both cards are standard MasterCards.

**cruise, the first all-women**
Olivia Records' first, February 12–16, 1990. The four-day Caribbean cruise sold out so quickly that Olivia added a second cruise on its heels, running February 19–23. Six hundred passengers sailed on each, visiting Key West, Nassau, and a private island called the Blue Lagoon.

**dentist, the first American to come out as gay**
Don Klein, now of Berkeley, California, believes that he was the first dentist to come out as a homosexual in the U.S. He did so in 1974, disclosing his homosexuality to the Utah State Dental Board, which twice told him it "would not license someone whom they knew was a practicing homosexual."

### doll, the first gay

Gay Bob. Produced by Out of the Closet, Inc., in 1978, the "anatomically correct" doll was sold wearing a plaid shirt, jeans, boots, and an earring.

### donation, the largest made to AIDS organizations

Fifteen percent of the $25-million Michael Bennett estate. When director-choreographer Michael Bennett died as a result of AIDS in July 1987, he left fifteen percent of his estate to be distributed to organizations "involved in the research of or the cure or treatment of patients afflicted with the disease known as AIDS." Previously, the largest receipt is believed to have been from the profits from Dionne Warwick's recording "That's What Friends Are For," which went to the American Foundation for AIDS Research (AmFAR).

### financial institution, the first gay-owned

Atlas Savings and Loan in San Francisco. Atlas opened in November 1981 with $3 million in assets; that figure jumped 188 percent to $8.65 million in six months. Savings deposits grew from $1 million to $5.5 million in the same period. Like many other savings and loans, however, Atlas sank into financial trouble because of millions of dollars' worth of bad loans, and had to close July 14, 1986.

### fire department, the first to establish a gay liaison position

The Boston Fire Department. The department created the part-time position in September 1988, to ease tensions with the local gay community after several incidents in which fire fighters harassed gays. An openly gay fire inspector, nine-year veteran Jim Murphy, was appointed to fill it.

**flag, the first gay**

A rainbow flag designed by Gilbert Baker of San Francisco in 1978. Inspired by rainbow flags flown by hippie groups in the 1960s, Baker designed one with eight stripes — from top to bottom, hot pink for sex, red for life, orange for healing, yellow for the sun, green for serenity with nature, turquoise for art, indigo for harmony, and violet for spirit — to be flown in San Francisco's 1978 Gay Freedom Day Parade. For the occasion, thirty volunteers hand-dyed and -stitched two enormous (forty-by-seventy-foot) flags. The rainbow flag caught on as a gay symbol over the next few years, with many variations in design. The design was more or less standardized by 1982, when the parade's organizing committee adopted it as a logo. By then, manufacturing limitations had resulted in the six-striped flag — red, orange, yellow, green, blue, and violet — commonly seen today.

**foundation, the first national to finance exclusively lesbian projects**

The Astraea National Lesbian Action Foundation, in New York. First called simply the Astraea Foundation, it was founded in 1977 by a multicultural, multiracial lesbian collective to fund primarily feminist projects. In 1990, it changed its name and its mission; it now gives $150,000 to $175,000 per year exclusively to progressive social-change and cultural projects relating to lesbians.

**fund-raiser, the first in the U.S. for a gay civil rights cause**

A benefit performance by Lester Horton's dance troupe in Los Angeles on May 23, 1952. Though not explicitly advertised as a benefit, most attendees knew the proceeds from the night — about $500 — were going to help the Mattachine Society fight the Dale Jennings case and the practice of entrapment.

**gathering, the largest gay and lesbian of all time**

The second March on Washington for Gay and Lesbian Rights, held October 11, 1987. Estimates of the size of the crowd ranged from the Park Service's conservative 200,000 to as high as 650,000, making it the largest assembly of gay people ever, as well as the largest gay rights demonstration ever. That weekend also marked the first public showing of the Names Project AIDS Memorial Quilt.

**Gay Games, the first**

Held in San Francisco in August 1982. Thirteen hundred male and female athletes participated in sixteen sports. The attendant arts festival featured more than twenty events, including dance, theatre, and art exhibits. The Gay Games were founded by physician and former Olympic decathlete Tom Waddell and organized by San Francisco Arts and Athletics, Inc.

**gay man or lesbian, the best-read**

Richard Labonté, who manages the Different Light bookstores on the West Coast, for many years managed to read every gay and lesbian book that was published in English, except for a few that he started but deemed not worth finishing. He estimates that he now reads about 60 percent of the total output, which is still about 400 books a year.

***Gayellow Pages,* the first**

Published in 1973.

### hall of fame, the first gay and lesbian

Chicago's Gay and Lesbian Hall of Fame, which inducted its first honorees June 26, 1991, as part of Gay Pride Week. Chicago is the first municipality to have initiated such an honor, each year recognizing the achievements of gays and lesbians who have contributed significantly to the betterment of the city of Chicago. Thus far, nearly thirty individuals and organizations have been honored.

### HIV-status identification card, the first

Partners for AIDS-Free America (PAFA), a Washington, D.C., company, created this identification card, which certifies the bearer as HIV-negative. To qualify, an applicant must take a completed application to a doctor or clinic and submit to a blood test. The doctor sends the results to PAFA; if negative, the company issues a laminated card for a $29.95 fee. The company also sells framed HIV-negative wall certificates to doctors and dentists for $75.95. The company began selling its ID cards in December 1991.

### humor album, the first commercially produced homophile

*Out of the Closets*, produced in early 1978 by Bob Booker, George Foster, and Bruce Vilanch, and distributed by Ariola America Records. The record featured a collection of comedic skits centered on gay and lesbian characters.

**jail rape survivor, the first male to go public**
Stephen Donaldson, in 1973. Arrested at the White House
in August 1973 for protesting U.S. bombing in Cambodia,
Donaldson, a Quaker, was held in the D.C. jail for over a
week. After being transferred — perhaps deliberately — from
a "quiet" cellblock, he was raped about sixty times by 45–50
men over a two-day period, August 21–22, 1973, in what is the
largest known male-male gang rape. Donaldson talked about
the experience in a press conference August 24 "in the hope"
that rapes of inmates could be prevented in the future.

**law enforcement agency, the first to encourage gay officers
to come out**
The San Francisco Police Department, in 1976.

**law enforcement officer, the first openly gay**
Rudi Cox. San Francisco Sheriff Richard Hongisto, who had encouraged Cox to apply for the job, hired the openly gay black
recruit as a deputy in 1976. As part of his training Cox had to
endure anti-gay texts and instructors who taught that homosexuals recruited teenagers and posed a threat to civilization.

**law enforcement officer, the first openly lesbian**
Denise Kreps. When Kreps applied in 1979 to become a
deputy sheriff in Contra Costa County, California, Sheriff
Richard Rainey refused to hire her because she was a lesbian.
Kreps took her case to court and won; the judge ruled in 1980
that Rainey had failed to provide "any evidence other than
speculative that showed that she couldn't do the job." Kreps
was hired, and graduated at the top of her training class the
following year, the first woman to do so.

**lesbian, the first open to be listed in the *Who's Who of American Women***

Jeanne Cordova, in the 1979–1980 edition. Among her accomplishments the entry listed her as founder, publisher, and editor of the *Lesbian Tide;* a member of the Gay Community Services Center board of directors; and a member of the National Lesbian Feminist Organization.

**lesbian, the first to reach the North Pole by dogsled**

Ann Bancroft, on May 1, 1986, after a grueling two-month trip from Ellesmere Island, Canada. She was also the first woman to do so.

**liaison, the first gay in the U.S.**

Ernest O. Reaugh. Reaugh was appointed in 1975 by New York State senator Manfred Ohrenstein to act as liaison to the gay community. He is believed to have been the first person to be appointed to such a position by any public official in the U.S.

**mail-order catalog, the first national gay and lesbian general-merchandise**

Shocking Grey. This company was the first to market general merchandise directly to the gay and lesbian community through a national mail-order catalog.

## march, the first gay pride

June 28, 1970, in New York City. Several thousand gay men and lesbians paraded up Sixth Avenue to celebrate the first anniversary of the Stonewall riots, declared Christopher Street Liberation Day by the Eastern Regional Conference of Homophile Organizations. The march ended in a "gay-in" in Central Park, where participants held hands, kissed, and smoked pot. Demonstrations were also held in Chicago, San Francisco, and Los Angeles.

## march, the first statewide gay rights in the U.S.

March 14, 1971, in Albany, New York. Some 3,500 protesters marched on the New York state capitol to demand an end to laws that discriminate against lesbians and gay men.

## March on Washington for Gay and Lesbian Rights, the first

October 14, 1979. An estimated 50,000 to 100,000 lesbians, gay men, and supporters attended, though the national news media virtually ignored the event. The same weekend as the march, hundreds participated in the first National Lesbian/Gay Third World Conference, also in D.C.

## Mardi Gras krewe, the first formally organized gay

Yuga-Duga, formed in 1959. Though the police raided its first ball and it lasted only three years, other gay krewes immediately followed in its wake.

### memorial, the largest AIDS

The Names Project AIDS Memorial Quilt. Begun in 1987 by Cleve Jones to commemorate the death of his best friend, the Quilt consists of individual three-by-six-foot panels, each bearing the name of a person lost to AIDS. When first displayed in October 1987 in Washington, D.C. (in conjunction with the first national March on Washington), it comprised nearly 2,000 panels. Shown in its entirety again in D.C. October 10–12, 1992, the quilt covered 12.9 acres (with walkways; 8.3 acres without) and included 22,000 panels. It has, of course, grown since then and may be the largest memorial of any kind in the world. It is undoubtedly the world's largest collectively made work of art.

### motorcade, the first gay

May 21, 1966, in Los Angeles. Thirteen cars traveled some twenty miles through the city with gay slogans painted on their sides. The picket-on-wheels was part of nationwide demonstrations held on Armed Services Day to protest the U.S. military's discrimination against homosexuals. The demonstrations were coordinated by NACHO; activist Harry Hay led the Los Angeles planning committee. The motorcade has also been called the first gay pride parade.

### National Coming Out Day, the first

October 11, 1988. National Coming Out Day was the creation of a group of some 200 lesbian and gay activists who met at the so-called War Conference in Virginia in February 1988 to determine a national strategy for gay rights. They chose October 11 in part because it marked the first showing of the Names Project AIDS Memorial Quilt; it is also, fortuitously, the birthday of Eleanor Roosevelt.

**organization, the first Asian gay in North America**
Boston Asian Gay Men and Lesbians (BAGMAL), begun in
1979.

**organization, the first bisexual rights**
National Bisexual Liberation, in New York. Donald Fass wrote
in a 1975 issue of *Bisexual Liberation* that he founded the
group in the spring of 1972.

**organization, the first documented homosexual rights in
North America**
The Society for Human Rights. Founded by a group of seven
men led by Henry Gerber, the organization was chartered by
the state of Illinois December 10, 1924. Its stated purpose was
"to promote and to protect the interests of people who by
reasons of mental and physical abnormalities are abused and
hindered in the legal pursuit of happiness ... and to combat
the public prejudices against them." The society managed to
publish two issues of a newsletter, *Friendship and Freedom*,
but its activities ended in 1925 after Gerber and two other
members were arrested without a warrant. Though Gerber's
case was dismissed, he lost his postal job and this meant the
end of the society.

**organization, the first gay and lesbian professional in the
U.S.**
The Gay and Lesbian Task Force of the American Library Association, formed in 1970. Originally called the Task Force on
Gay Liberation, and later the Gay Task Force, it was initiated
by librarians Janet Cooper and Israel Fishman as part of the
ALA's Social Responsibilities Round Table. As Barbara Gittings
has noted, this was "the first time that gay people in any
professional association openly banded together to advance
the gay cause through that profession."

**organization, the first (and oldest) lesbian in North America**
Daughters of Bilitis (DOB), officially founded in San Francisco on October 19, 1955 by four lesbian couples, who had begun meeting September 21 to discuss forming a social club. One of those founding couples, Del Martin and Phyllis Lyon, was instrumental in turning the DOB into a national rallying point for lesbians. The DOB began publishing the *Ladder* in October 1956, continuing without break for sixteen years. There are still active DOB chapters across the country.

**organization, the first interracial gay**
The Knights of the Clock, founded in Los Angeles in June 1950 or earlier by Merton Bird, a black gay man, to promote understanding between black and white gays and to provide support for interracial gay couples.

**organization, the first professional to condemn anti-gay discrimination**
The American Sociological Association, which in September 1969 issued a statement condemning "the firing, taking economic sanctions, and other oppressive actions against any persons for reasons of sexual preference."

### organization, the first successful gay rights in North America

The Mattachine Society, founded in Los Angeles in 1951.
Though Harry Hay first conceived of organizing homosexuals
in 1948, the Mattachine Society didn't begin forming until
1950, when Hay met Rudi Gernreich, and the two in turn con-
nected with Bob Hull, Chuck Rowland, and Dale Jennings.
The five began meeting weekly in November 1950. When Kon-
rad Stevens and James Gruber joined the five in April 1951,
their efforts coalesced and the Mattachine Society was born,
spawning chapters across the country. Acting on the theory
that homosexuals are an oppressed minority, the Mattachine
Society set in motion the first wave of the homosexual rights
movement in the United States. It gradually died in the wake
of the radical activism sparked by the Stonewall riots.

### organization, the largest lesbian in the U.S.

Bay Area Career Women, with a membership of 1,400 to
1,500. Nicole Schapiro founded this professional and social organization in 1980. Incorporated in 1983, it now has six chapters in the Bay Area. Its donation-supported BACW Fund helps
finance a variety of lesbian and feminist projects.

### organization, the oldest American gay

ONE, Inc., founded in Los Angeles in October 15, 1952, as the
publisher of the monthly *ONE Magazine.* Though the organization suffered many splits over the years, among those at the
heart of its success were Dorr Legg, Don Slater, and Jim Kepner. *ONE Magazine* ceased regular publication in 1969, but
ONE, Inc., continues today as an educational institute and
resource center.

### organization, the world's oldest gay

The Nederlandse Vereniging tot Integratie van Homoseksualiteit COC [Dutch Alliance for the Integration of Homosexuality] in Amsterdam. Originally called the Amsterdam Shakespeare Club by its founders — the editors of the gay magazine *Levensrecht* [*Right to Live*] — this group held its first meeting December 8–9, 1946. It became the COC (Cultuur en Ontspannings Centrum, or Culture and Recreation Center) some two years later, taking its current name in 1971. Primarily a social organization, it has some 7,000 members and centers in forty cities throughout the Netherlands.

### Oscar winner, the first lesbian to acknowledge her partner in her acceptance speech

Debra Chasnoff. Chasnoff won an Academy Award March 30, 1992, for her documentary short film *Deadly Deception: General Electric, Nuclear Weapons and Our Environment.* Besides thanking her lover of twelve years, Kim Klausner, on national television, Chasnoff urged the audience to boycott General Electric.

### panel, the first in the Names Project AIDS Memorial Quilt

One commemorating Marvin Feldman, the best friend of Names Project founder Cleve Jones. Feldman's death from AIDS in the fall of 1986 left Jones devastated for months. Then, one day, while reminiscing about friends they'd lost to AIDS, Jones and a friend began painting names and designs on a piece of fabric with paints they'd found in the garage. Jones found the experience so therapeutic that he invited others to join him in creating a giant quilt of such panels, commemorating those lost to AIDS.

**paper currency, the first to portray a recognized lesbian**
Sweden's new twenty-crown note, issued in 1992. The note features the novelist Selma Lagerlöf, who in 1909 was the first woman to receive the Nobel Prize for literature. Lagerlöf had a long relationship with another writer, Sophie Elkan.

**physician, the first openly gay American**
Dr. Howard Brown. New York City's former commissioner of health came out in a front-page interview in the *New York Times* on October 2, 1973.

**postmark, the first gay**
Sweden, in 1983, was the first country to use a gay slogan to cancel stamps. The cancellation read "Gay Pride Week" and showed the lambda symbol. In the United States, members of GLAAD (Gay and Lesbian Alliance Against Defamation), using Keith Haring's "Gay Pride" drawing, designed a cancellation that was used June 25, 1989, Gay Pride Day, in New York. The U.S. Postal Service set up a table on Christopher Street and canceled thousands of pieces of mail that day with the message "Stonewall Sta., 20 years 1969–1989, Lesbian and Gay Pride, June 25, 1989, New York, NY 10199."

**psychiatrist, the first openly gay**
Dr. Richard Pillard, a professor of psychiatry at Boston University School of Medicine. Pillard was asked by Dr. Howard Brown, the first American physician to come out as gay, to be included in an article on gay physicians published in *Medical World News* in late 1973 or early 1974. Pillard was also the first psychiatrist to push through a resolution (in the Massachusetts chapter of the American Psychiatric Association) to remove homosexuality from the *Diagnostic and Statistical Manual,* the bible of the mental health trade.

### PWA, the first gay to go public

Bobbi Campbell, in the *Sentinel,* a San Francisco gay newspaper, on December 10, 1981. With the words "I'm Bobbi Campbell and I have 'gay cancer,'" this registered nurse, the sixteenth San Francisco resident to be diagnosed with Kaposi's sarcoma, launched a personal campaign to raise awareness of the disease among San Francisco gays. He proclaimed himself the "KS Poster Boy."

### PWA, the first to address a national political convention

Keith Gann. Gann spoke at the 1988 Democratic National Convention in Atlanta. An openly gay alternate delegate from St. Paul, Minnesota, he spoke in support of the Democrats' platform on AIDS.

### PWA, the first to run a marathon

Marc A. Hein, at the Vancouver Gay Games III, August 11, 1990. Hein, a 41-year-old architect and activist from Kansas City, completed the 26.2 miles in 4 hours, 35 minutes. Four years earlier, just two months after being diagnosed as HIV-positive, he had run the Gay Games II marathon.

### rodeo, the first gay

1976, in Reno, Nevada.

### stamp, the first (and only) to show a pair of same-sex lovers

One of the "Surrender at Cornwallis" sheet, showing Alexander Hamilton with his purported lover Colonel John Laurens. This appears to be the only stamp to show two same-sex lovers together, though on October 27, 1951, the French postal department issued a set of stamps featuring, individually, lovers Paul Verlaine and Arthur Rimbaud.

### stamp club, the first gay

The Gay and Lesbian History on Stamps Club. Though there may have been a gay stamp club in Germany before World War II, the GLHSC is the first to collect stamps featuring gay people. Founded by Paul Hennefeld, Blair O'Dell, and Brian Lanter in 1982, the club was not accepted as an official study unit by the American Topical Association until June 1985. The GLHSC was also the first gay organization in the United States to have its logo designed by an official government agency — the U.S. Postal Service, for the 1989 World Stamp EXPO exhibit.

### stamp collection, the first gay to be publicly exhibited

"Alternate Lifestyles of Famous People: A Gay and Lesbian Philatelic Collection." Assembled by Paul Hennefeld, it was first displayed at a stamp show at the Coliseum in New York in March 1983, where it won a bronze award. Its first official exhibition was at Interplex '83, also at the Coliseum, under the shortened title "Alternate Lifestyles ... Out of the Closet." The collection won its first National Gold Award on Gay Pride Day, 1987.

### telephone listing, the first to contain the word *gay*

The listing for the Gay Liberation Front of the Tri-Cities (Albany, New York), now the Lesbian and Gay Community Service Center, in July 1970.

### tennis player, the winningest lesbian

Martina Navratilova, who has won at least seventeen Grand Slam singles titles (and countless double titles) in her career, including a Grand Slam in 1984 and nine Wimbledon Championships. Navratilova was the first tennis player ever to win this many Wimbledons.

**wedding, the largest gay**

October 10, 1987, in Washington, D.C. Two thousand gay and lesbian couples exchanged vows on the steps of the Internal Revenue Service building. The mass ceremony was part of a week of activities and demonstrations planned in conjunction with the 1987 March on Washington for Gay and Lesbian Rights.

# EDUCATION

### college, the first to ban ROTC in protest of the military's anti-gay policies

Pitzer College in Claremont, California. Pitzer's faculty-student college council passed a resolution April 12, 1990, banning future ROTC (Resident Officers Training Corps) scholarships and credit for military science classes, effective the fall of 1991. The resolution stated: "Pitzer College has taken this action out of the conviction that the current policies practiced by the ROTC, which discriminate against gays and lesbians in military service, are unconscionable and are in direct conflict with Pitzer's commitment not to discriminate on the basis of sexual preference."

### dance, the first college-level homosexual

The "First NYC All-College Gay Mixer," in the spring of 1969. Sponsored by the NYU and Columbia chapters of the Student Homophile League, the dance was held in the parish hall of the Church of the Holy Apostles and drew a crowd of several hundred.

### fraternity, the first gay

Delta Lambda Phi. Based in Washington, D.C., this fraternity was not originally associated with any school. In March 1988, however, UCLA approved a chapter of the fraternity, just one month after it officially recognized the nation's first lesbian sorority. Four other universities, including the University of Minnesota, soon followed suit.

### gay studies course, the first

An interdisciplinary course taught at the University of Nebraska in the fall of 1970 appears to have been the first. Offered jointly by the sociology, anthropology, and English departments and taught by Louis Compton, the course focused primarily on the civil rights of homosexuals but included a critique of the sickness theory.

### graduate school, the first gay

ONE Institute in Los Angeles, founded as an educational institute in 1956 and recognized as a graduate school by the state of California in 1981. It offers a Ph.D. in homophile studies and thus far has awarded two, as well as four master's degrees and four honorary doctorates.

### high school, the first gay

Byton High, in Philadelphia. The school was started in 1982 for gay teens as an alternative to the public high school system. Its first graduates, the class of '83, consisted of one female student and three males.

### high schools, the first to officially recognize gay student groups

George Washington High School in Manhattan and the Bronx High School of Science. In the spring of 1973, these two became the first known public high schools to officially recognize gay student groups. Both groups were formed after representatives from the Gay Activists Alliance's Agitprop Committee spoke at classes and assemblies at each school.

**high school student, the first to take a same-sex date to a prom**

Seventeen-year-old Randy Rohl, of Sioux Falls, South Dakota, in June 1979. Aaron Fricke, a Rhode Island high school student, received nationwide media attention when he went to court the next year for the right to do the same.

**organization, the first (and oldest) gay campus**

The Student Homophile League at Columbia University, founded in 1966 by a bisexual undergraduate, Robert A. Martin, now known as Stephen Donaldson. The group held its first formal program October 28, 1966. On April 19, 1967, the university issued a charter officially recognizing the group as a campus organization. Immediately publicizing that recognition to make it politically irreversible, Martin then worked to establish chapters at New York University (chaired by Rita Mae Brown) and Cornell (chaired by Gerald Moldenhauer, later of *Body Politic* renown, under the sponsorship of the Reverend Phil Berrigan). The Columbia group, though it has gone through several name changes, is still going, and recently celebrated its twenty-fifth anniversary.

**school board, the first in the U.S. to ban anti-gay discrimination**

The District of Columbia school board, in May 1972. At the urging of the local Gay Activists Alliance, the board enacted a resolution prohibiting discrimination in any aspect of the D.C. school system's hiring practices. Gay teachers' rights were reaffirmed the following year when a more general human rights law — Title 34 — was passed, prohibiting discrimination in educational institutions and all other employment.

### school district, the first in the U.S. to ban discrimination against gay students

Santa Barbara, California. The board of education voted December 15, 1977, to broaden its policy of nondiscrimination against gay teachers and other gay school employees to include gay students. It also established a grievance procedure for handling cases of discrimination against employees or students.

### sorority, the first lesbian

Lambda Delta Lambda, at the University of California, Los Angeles. With nine founding members, the sorority won official recognition from UCLA in February 1988.

### student body president, the first openly gay at a major university

Jack Baker, a law student and gay activist, elected president of the University of Minnesota's 34,000 students in April 1971. Baker received 46 percent of the votes in the five-way race.

### university, the first gay

Lavender U, A University for Gay Women and Gay Men. Founded by a collective of seven gay men and two lesbians, Lavender U offered its first classes in San Francisco in January 1974. Classes, which included such offerings as Gay Greek Literature I and II, A Rose Is a Rose Is a Rose, The Bath Experience, and Opera Appreciation, were taught out of private homes or at public facilities. Enrollment from its first catalog was about 200.

# RELIGION

### church, the first documented gay

The Church of ONE Brotherhood. Founded in Los Angeles in 1956 by Chuck Rowland, it lasted only a year. Often cited as the first gay church is the Metropolitan Community Church, founded in Los Angeles in October 1968 by the Reverend Troy Perry, a gay Pentacostal minister.

### congregation, the world's largest lesbian and gay

The Cathedral of Hope Metropolitan Community Church, Dallas, Texas. The Cathedral of Hope has 892 active members and more than 2,100 constituent members. Its average attendance is over 750 people per week, and it had 1,333 people gather for Easter 1992. It has also undertaken the largest construction effort of any lesbian and gay organization: a $2.5-million, 26,300-square-foot building that will seat more than 1,000 people, set on six acres in the heart of Dallas.

### denomination, the first to establish a lesbian and gay office

Unitarian Universalists, in 1973. Three years earlier, the general assembly had passed a resolution banning discrimination against gays in the church.

### denomination, the first to perform gay and lesbian union ceremonies

Unitarian Universalists, in 1984.

### minister, the first openly gay ordained

William Johnson. Ordained June 25, 1972, by the United Church of Christ in San Carlos, California, Johnson was the first open homosexual to be ordained by a major Christian denomination. He came out in 1970 while a student at the Pacific School of Religion in Berkeley, California. He now serves as secretary for AIDS Programs and Ministries Coordination at the UCC denominational headquarters in Cleveland.

### minister, the first openly lesbian

Ellen Marie Barrett. Barrett was the first open lesbian to be ordained by a major Christian denomination. She was ordained as an Episcopal priest January 10, 1977, in Manhattan, New York City.

### rabbi, the first openly gay

Allen Bennett. Bennett became a rabbi in 1974, then moved to San Francisco in 1977 to continue his postgraduate studies. There, he joined a gay synagogue, Congregation Sha'ar Zahav, becoming the rabbi there in 1979. He was outed, with his permission, by the *San Francisco Examiner* in November 1978.

### organization, the first bisexual religious

The Committee of Friends on Bisexuality, officially founded by Stephen Donaldson (a.k.a. Robert Martin) on June 29, 1973, in Ithaca, New York. The group first gathered in June 1972, issuing a statement, the "Ithaca Statement on Bisexuality," which appears to be the first statement on bisexuality — and is undoubtedly the first pro-bi declaration — by any religious body. The committee ended in 1977.

**organization, the first denominational religious for homosexuals**

Dignity, an organization of Catholic gays and lesbians that began as a rap group in San Diego in 1969, then moved to Los Angeles, where the first chapter was founded in 1970.

**organization, the first gay religious**

The Council on Religion and the Homosexual, founded in San Francisco in December 1964 by the Reverend Ted McIlvenna and other clergy members "to promote continuing dialogue between the church and the homosexual."

**organization, the first gay religious of any kind to be officially recognized by a national body**

Beth Chayim Chadashim in Los Angeles, the first synagogue, founded in 1972. It received its charter from the Union of American Hebrew Congregations July 19, 1974.

**organization, the largest gay religious**

Dignity, with 6,000 due-paying members and as many as three times that number participating in its services and activities.

**synagogue, the first gay**

Beth Chayim Chadashim in Los Angeles, founded in 1972. The synagogue was formed after two gay men and two lesbians attending a rap session at the Los Angeles Metropolitan Community Church in April 1972 discovered they were all Jewish and decided to form a temple of their own. Continuing to meet at MCC till it burned, they held their first service in July 1972 and were chartered two years later by the Union of American Hebrew Congregations. In 1977 the congregation acquired its own building, dedicated in 1981.

**synagogue, the largest gay**

Congregation Beth Simchat Torah in New York. Founded in 1973, this, the second gay synagogue in the U.S., is the largest in the world, with more than a thousand members.

# POLITICS

### candidate, the first openly gay for public office

José Sarria. A legendary drag queen known as the Dowager Widow of the Emperor Norton, Empress of San Francisco, and Protectress of Mexico, Sarria received 5,600 votes when he ran for the position of San Francisco city supervisor in 1961.

### candidate, the first openly gay for the U.S. Congress

Frank Kameny. Kameny, an astrophysicist and founder and president of the Mattachine Society's Washington chapter, announced his candidacy for the District of Columbia's first congressional seat February 3, 1971, and was one of four (out of twenty-five) independents to get enough signatures to get on the ballot. In the March 23 election, won by black Democrat Walter Fauntroy, Kameny garnered 1,841 votes, 1.6 percent of the total, coming in fourth in the six-way race, ahead of candidates from the Black United Front and the Socialist Workers Party.

### candidate, the first openly gay for the vice-presidential nomination

Melvin Boozer, in 1980. The seventy-six gay delegates attending the 1980 Democratic National Convention in New York gathered enough signatures to nominate Boozer, a black gay activist from D.C., for vice-president. Activist Bill Kraus of San Francisco and former National Gay Task Force director Virginia Apuzzo gave nominating speeches. Addressing the convention, Boozer said there was no difference between the discrimination he experienced as an African-American and that he experienced as a gay man. The Carter-Mondale ticket prevailed.

**candidate, the first U.S. presidential to mention gays in his acceptance speech**

Bill Clinton, accepting the Democratic nomination at the Democratic National Convention July 16, 1992. "For too long, politicians have told us that what's wrong with America is the rest of us. Them. Them the minorities. Them the liberals. Them the gays," he said. The inclusion came after gay and lesbian activists, having obtained a copy of a draft that made no mention of gays or lesbians, lobbied the campaign just shortly before Clinton gave the speech.

**city, the first "gay"**

West Hollywood, California. This community of 35,000 people, 40 percent of whom were estimated to be gay or lesbian, was incorporated as a city November 6, 1984, with a gay majority on its city council and a lesbian mayor. As one of its first acts, the council passed a sweeping gay rights ordinance. In 1991, the council had one gay member.

**city, the first to officially proclaim a gay pride week**

Ann Arbor, Michigan. In 1972, just weeks before passing the nation's first comprehensive gay civil rights law, Ann Arbor's city council officially declared June 19–26 Gay Pride Week, approving 6 to 4 a resolution drafted by the Ann Arbor Gay Liberation Front.

**civil disobedience action, the largest gay**

October 13, 1987, in Washington, D.C. Six hundred protestors allowed themselves to be arrested on the steps of the Supreme Court in protest of the Court's upholding of sodomy laws.

**delegates, the first openly gay to a national convention**
Jim Foster of San Francisco and Madeline Davis of Buffalo,
New York. On July 12, 1972, at the Democratic National
Convention in Miami, where party delegates had gathered to
nominate Senator George McGovern as the Democratic presidential candidate, Foster became the first openly gay person to
address the national convention of a major party. Davis also
spoke.

**demonstration, the first American against the "sickness"
theory**
On April 23, 1968, the Student Homophile League of Columbia
University picketed and leafleted and infiltrated a panel of
psychiatrists discussing homosexuality at an event sponsored
by the Columbia University College of Physicians and
Surgeons.

**demonstration, the first American gay rights**
A picket protesting unfair treatment of gays by the military.
Organized in 1963 by activist Randy Wicker of the Homosexual League of New York, the picket was held at the Whitehall
Street Induction Center in New York to protest violation of the
confidentiality of homosexuals' draft records. Fewer than a
dozen people participated. Conflicting sources date the September 19 picket as 1963 or 1964. Often cited as the first gay
rights demonstration in the U.S. is a picket held at the United
Nations headquarters in New York on Easter Sunday, 1965.
Some twenty-five Mattachine members picketed to protest the
news that Castro planned to round up Cuban homosexuals
and put them in work camps.

**demonstration, the first gay rights to be held at the White House**
A May 29, 1965, picket sponsored by ECHO. Seven men and three women participated, including activist Frank Kameny, organizer Jack Nichols, and Lilli Vincenz, the sole lesbian. The picket received nationwide television coverage.

**elected official, the first openly gay**
Kathy Kozachenko. Running as a member of the Human Rights Party, she was elected to the Ann Arbor, Michigan, City Council in 1974. She was not the first gay person to serve on the council, however: the previous fall, two outgoing council members who had been elected in 1972, Nancy Wechsler and Gerald DeGrieck, had come out as gay.

**elected official, the first openly gay at the national level**
Congressman Gerry Studds (D-Massachusetts). Studds came out July 14, 1983, after a House Ethics committee recommended that he be reprimanded for having an affair with a seventeen-year-old House page ten years earlier. Six days later, the House voted to officially censure him. The first national-level American elected official to come out completely voluntarily was Congressman Barney Frank (D-Massachusetts), who did so May 30, 1987, in an interview in the *Boston Globe*.

**elected official, the first openly gay black**
Keith St. John. A lawyer in Albany, N.Y., St. John was elected to the city's common council in 1989, winning by a 4-to-1 margin over his closest opponent.

**elected official, the first openly gay in a major U.S. city**
Harvey Milk. Milk was elected to the San Francisco Board of Supervisors November 8, 1977.

### elected official, the first openly gay Republican

Robert Ebersole, the town clerk of Lunenberg, Massachusetts. He came out in 1984 and later easily won re-election.

### elected official, the first openly gay state

Elaine Noble. Elected November 5, 1974, to the Massachusetts House of Representatives, Noble was the first to win election to a state office. She was not, however, the first to *hold* a state office: On December 9, encouraged by Noble's victory but before she took office, Minnesota State senator Allan Spear publicly declared his homosexuality.

### elected official, the first openly lesbian black

Sherry Harris. Harris "ran away" with the Seattle City Council election in November 1991, winning 67 percent of the vote to become the first black open lesbian in U.S. history to win a political office.

### governor, the first to sign an executive order giving gay and lesbian state workers bereavement and family leave

Governor William Weld of Massachusetts. Weld signed the order September 23, 1992. The order grants gay and lesbian state workers at the management level the same bereavement and family leave rights that heterosexual workers are allowed when their partners are sick or have died.

### judge, the first openly gay

Stephen M. Lachs. Then-California governor Jerry Brown appointed Lachs to a spot on the Los Angeles Superior Court on September 17, 1979. Previously, Lachs had been a juvenile court commissioner.

### judge, the first openly lesbian

Mary Morgan, appointed August 26, 1981, to the San Francisco Municipal Court by then-California governor Jerry Brown.

### judge, the first openly lesbian elected

Donna Hitchens. Hitchens was the first open lesbian in the country to be elected to a superior court judgeship. Her 1990 victory also made her the highest-ranking openly gay elected official in California.

### knight, England's first openly gay

Ian McKellen. Queen Elizabeth II knighted the famed Shakespearean actor on New Year's Eve, 1990, in recognition of his pre-eminence in the arts. McKellen was chosen for the honor by former prime minister Margaret Thatcher's administration shortly before she left office, and some gay activists thought he should refuse knighthood in protest of the anti-gay Tory administration. Others called it "a significant landmark in the history of the British Gay Movement."

### mayor, the first openly gay in the U.S.

Gerald E. Ulrich, elected mayor of Bunceton, Missouri, in 1980.

### mayor, the first openly lesbian in England

Margaret Roff of Manchester, England, elected mayor by the city's Labour Party council on November 13, 1985. Roff, a prominent gay rights activist, declined the title of "lord mayor," preferring to refer to herself as "chair."

**mayor, the first openly lesbian in the U.S.**

Valerie Terrigno, of West Hollywood, California, in 1984. The top vote-getter among the five city council members, she became mayor a month after her election to the council. She later resigned and was convicted of embezzling government funds while operating an employment and housing agency.

**member of Parliament, Canada's first openly gay**

Svend Robinson, first elected in 1979. Though Robinson never hid his sexuality, and had long been outspoken on gay issues, on February 29, 1988, he came out on national television, on the CBC French-language information show "Le Point." An hour later, he was speaking with host Barbara Frum on "The Journal," a top-rated English-language current affairs program, explaining gay rights issues to a million and a half Canadians. A New Democrat, he had represented the Burnaby district east of Vancouver since 1979. His announcement made him one of only four openly gay elected national politicians in the world.

**member of Parliament, Italy's first openly gay**

Niki Vendola, elected in April 1992. A Communist, Vendola represents the Apulia region of Italy, where his constituency consists primarily of blue-collar workers and peasants.

**member of Parliament, the U.K.'s first openly gay**

Chris Smith, elected in 1983, representing the Islington borough of London. Smith came out November 10, 1984, in the town of Rugby, England, while addressing a demonstration protesting a proposal by the town to ban gay employees. Afterward his Labour Party colleagues in the House of Commons collected signatures of support for his action; not a single Labour MP refused to sign.

**organization, the first explicitly gay to be granted tax-exempt status**

The Homosexual Information Center, in Universal City, California, in 1968. The first group with *gay* actually in its name to win such recognition was the Gay Community Services Center of Los Angeles, which won its tax-exempt status as a charitable, nonprofit corporation August 14, 1974, after a three-year fight.

**party platform, the first U.S. to feature a gay rights plank**

The 1980 Democratic platform. Adopted June 24, 1980, under a Carter-Mondale ticket, it advocated support for the rights of various minority groups, including blacks, Hispanics, American Indians, Americans living abroad, and homosexuals. Gay activist Sheldon Andelson introduced the plank at the convention.

**president, the first U.S. to sign into law a bill specifically mentioning "sexual orientation"**

President George Bush, on April 23, 1990, when he signed the Hate Crimes Statistics Act, ordering a five-year study of crimes motivated by hatred for a victim's "race, religion, sexual orientation, or ethnicity." Representatives of the National Gay and Lesbian Task Force and the Human Rights Campaign Fund were invited to the White House ceremony only after they agreed not to use the event to protest Bush's policy on federal funding of AIDS research and treatment. This is said to have been the first time gay rights activists were invited as such to an official White House action.

### presidential administration, the first U.S. to receive a gay and lesbian delegation

Jimmy Carter's, in 1977. White House aide Midge Costanza, acting as community liaison for Carter, received the first official gay and lesbian delegation to the White House on February 8, meeting with officers of the National Gay Task Force to discuss ways the administration could further the cause of gay rights. Six weeks later, a second meeting was held, this time with two dozen gay rights advocates.

### presidential appointee, the first openly gay

Dr. Frank Lilly, appointed by President Ronald Reagan to the Presidential Commission on the Human Immunodeficiency Virus Epidemic in the summer of 1987. Many other appointees to the commission were right-wing ideologues with little or no AIDS-related experience or knowledge.

### protest, the first nationwide of an anti-gay media portrayal

Coordinated by the National Gay Task Force in the fall of 1974 over an episode of "Marcus Welby, M.D." called "The Outrage," which ABC broadcast October 8. In it a junior high school student is raped by his male science teacher. Protesters condemned the show for fostering "a false and negative stereotype of homosexuals" as child molesters. Dozens of prominent officials, including representatives of the United Federation of Teachers and the American Psychiatric Association, joined the protest. ABC ran the show anyway, but several advertisers — including Bayer Aspirin, Listerine, Gallo Wine, and Ralston Purina — withdrew their support, five local affiliates refused to air it, and others allowed time for rebuttals by gay rights advocates.

### Republican organization, the first gay

The Log Cabin Republican Club. Initially called Gay Republicans of Southern California, this group first met September 1, 1977, in Los Angeles. Chartered as the Log Cabin Club by the state of California on August 6, 1979, it was officially recognized by the Los Angeles Republican party June 11, 1985. Its official purpose is twofold: to educate the gay community about the Republican party and to educate Republicans about the concerns of gay men and lesbians. The group now has twenty-eight chapters across the United States.

### union, the first in the U.S. to offer AIDS health care benefits

Local 2 of the San Francisco Hotel Employees and Restaurant Employees Union. In early 1991 the local set up a fund, expected to reach $4 million by 1994, to reimburse medical expenses not covered by regular health insurance. Members with HIV-related medical conditions can receive up to $350 per month to cover prescription and experimental drugs, insurance payments and deductibles, diagnostic and laboratory charges, licensed home and hospice care, and medical supplies and equipment, as well as rent, food, and transportation in emergency situations. Employers pay $5 per employee per month for the benefits in the first year, $10 per month in the second year, $15 in the third, and $20 in the fourth and subsequent years.

### union contract, the first gay

Unionized employees of the Gay and Lesbian Community Services Center of Los Angeles signed a three-year contract with GLCSC in December 1984, establishing them as the first gay and lesbian collective bargaining unit in the United States. The group is affiliated with the Service Employees International Union of the AFL-CIO.

# LAW

### bill, the first gay rights to be introduced in Congress

HR-14752, submitted to the House on May 14, 1974, by its sponsors, Representatives Bella Abzug and Edward Koch, both Democrats from New York. If passed, the bill would have added "sexual orientation, sex, or marital status" to the list of characteristics protected from discrimination under the 1964 Civil Rights Act.

### city, the first U.S. to ban discrimination in hiring

East Lansing, Michigan. East Lansing's city council voted March 7, 1972, to amend the city's personnel rules to ban discrimination against gays in hiring by the city. Though initially a provision to the amendment would still have allowed the city to dismiss employees for homosexual solicitation (as opposed to homosexuality per se), this provision was removed just two weeks later. Two months later, another Michigan city, Ann Arbor, passed an even broader gay rights amendment to its human rights code.

### city, the first U.S. to extend spousal benefits to gay city workers

Berkeley, California. On December 5, 1984, Berkeley became the first U.S. city to pass a "domestic partners" law for city employees. Gay, lesbian, and unmarried heterosexual couples could register with the city to receive benefits comparable to those married couples receive in areas such as health and dental care, bereavement leave, and leave to care for a sick partner.

**city, the first U.S. to include anti-gay language in its charter**
Springfield, Oregon. On May 19, 1992, the town's citizens
voted 5,693 to 4,540 to bar the town from protecting homosexuals from discrimination and to prohibit it from actions that
"promote, encourage, or facilitate" homosexuality, pedophilia,
or sadomasochism. Under the law, any city agency may deny
services to any gay organization or any nongay group that sup-
ports civil rights for gay people; public libraries must remove
items that treat homosexuality positively or neutrally; gay pride
events are banned from public property; and the city may not
pass or enforce any law that recognizes sexual orientation.
Voters in nearby Corvallis rejected an identical measure. Both
ballot measures were sponsored by the Oregon Citizen's Alliance, an extremist group working to pass even stronger initia-
tives statewide.

**city, the first U.S. to pass a broad gay civil rights law**
Ann Arbor, Michigan. On July 10, 1972, the city council passed
an amendment to the city's human rights code that made discrimination against gays in employment, housing, and public
accommodation illegal throughout the city.

**country, the first European to decriminalize homosexuality**
Denmark, in 1930.

**country, the first to pass a national gay rights law**
Norway. In 1981, King Olav V signed a comprehensive law
prohibiting "public statements that threaten or scorn a person
or group of persons, or expose anyone to hatred, persecution,
or contempt because of their homosexual orientation or life-
style." The law also made it illegal to refuse goods or services
to anyone on the basis of that person's sexual orientation.

**country, the first to protect the rights of gay and lesbian couples**
Sweden. In the summer of 1988 Sweden passed legislation protecting the rights of lesbian and gay couples with regard to tax breaks, inheritance, and certain social services.

**income tax refund, the first issued to a same-sex couple on a jointly filed federal return**
Given to Dick Leitsch and Robert Amsel of New York, though the year was not cited. In 1971, a lesbian couple, Neva Joy Heckman and Judith Ann Belew, received a refund check after filing a joint 1970 federal return.

**law, North America's first anti-sodomy**
The Virginia Colony decreed the death penalty for sodomites in 1610.

**law, the first U.S. affecting gay custody claims**
An ordinance passed by the District of Columbia City Council on June 28, 1976. The ordinance eliminated sex discriminatory language from sections of the district's legal code and stated that factors such as "sexual orientation," race, political affiliation, and sex "shall not be a conclusive consideration" in matters of custody and visitation.

### law, the first to recognize same-sex relationships

Bill 86, passed by the parliament of Quebec, Canada, December 18, 1982. The legislation was the first to give same-sex relationships equal legal status with heterosexual relationships, making same-sex couples eligible for various employee benefits, worker's compensation, and reduced insurance rates and requiring both private and public agencies to treat same-sex couples equally.

### legislative hearing, the first on gay rights

Held November 1970 at the New York Bar Association. It was called by Assemblymen Franz Lichter, Tony Olivieri, and Steve Solarz.

### litigation victory, the largest gay rights

A December 4, 1986, settlement between Pacific Bell and the National Gay Rights Advocates ending an eleven-year lawsuit over Pacific Bell's anti-gay employment policy. The settlement was expected to cost the company some $5 million.

### marriage, the first attempt in the U.S. at a legal gay

A ceremony performed June 12, 1970, to join Neva Joy Heckman and Judith Ann Belew. The Reverend Troy Perry performed the double-ring ceremony at the Los Angeles Metropolitan Community Church. Under California law, couples who have been together for two years or more may formalize a common-law marriage with a church ceremony and issuance of a church certificate, without needing a marriage license. Heckman and Belew had been together just over two years.

**marriage license application, the first same-sex in the U.S.**
Jack Baker and James Michael McConnell, in Minneapolis on
May 18, 1970. They were denied but filed suit. While the suit
was on appeal to the state supreme court, McConnell adopted
Baker in juvenile court; in the process, Baker had his legal
name changed to Pat Lyn McConnell. Mike McConnell then applied for and received a marriage license in Mankato, Minnesota, seventy-five miles away. Using this license, the two
were wed September 3, 1971, by a United Methodist minister.
A month later, the state supreme court upheld the denial of
their original application. Continuing to try to have their relationship legally recognized, Baker and McConnell filed joint
tax returns for 1972 and 1973, which the IRS accepted without
comment but the state rejected. In 1974, they applied to adopt
a child but appear to have been denied. They then sued the
Veterans Administration to have McConnell's rights as Baker's
dependent spouse recognized. By 1976, the couple had ex-
hausted their legal avenues for having their relationship legally
recognized.

**marriages, the world's first legally sanctioned same-sex**
Eleven couples gathered in Copenhagen, Denmark, on October 1, 1989, for the world's first legal gay marriages. Among
the couples were Axel Axgil, who founded Denmark's first gay
organization in 1948, and his life partner, Eigil Axgil.

**mass arrest, the largest of gay men in North America**
February 5, 1981, in Toronto, Canada. In a raid on four gay
bathhouses, police armed with crowbars and sledgehammers
arrested 305 men. The raids prompted a riot the following
night by more than 3,000 angry demonstrators. It was the
largest civilian mass arrest in Canada's history.

### military personnel, the first openly gay to be re-enlisted in the U.S. military

Sergeant Miriam ben-Shalom. Ben-Shalom first came out in 1976 in a military newspaper, while a member of the Army Reserves. After a long legal battle with the U.S. Army, a lower court finally ordered her reinstated, making her the first openly gay person to ever be re-enlisted by any branch of the U.S. military. That ruling was overturned in 1989 after the Army appealed, however, and in February 1990 ben-Shalom was left without further recourse when the Supreme Court refused to hear her appeal.

### mother, the first open lesbian to win custody of her children

Camille M. Mitchell of San Jose, California. Despite contentions by her husband of fifteen years that she was an "unfit mother," Mitchell won custody of her three children June 8, 1972, in divorce proceedings in Santa Clara County Superior Court. The decision was at best a hollow victory, however, as the conditions imposed by Superior Judge Gerald S. Chargin were appallingly restrictive: Mitchell was forbidden to live with her lesbian lover "at any time in the future" and, further, was allowed to see her lover only during daytime hours when the children were at school or visiting their father.

### palimony suit, the first gay

Filed by Randal Jones in July 1978. The male model and live-in lover of actor James Daly sued the Daly estate for $5 million after Daly's daughters evicted Jones after Daly's death.

**palimony suit, the first gay to be decided by a jury**

James Short was awarded more than $2 million in palimony by a San Francisco jury after he broke up with his lover of nineteen years. The September 9, 1987, decision is believed to have been the first to be handed down by a jury in a gay palimony case.

**palimony suit, the first lesbian**

On June 6, 1978, a San Diego Superior Court judge ordered Denease Conley to pay $100 per month in support to Sherry D. Richardson. The two had wed in a holy union ceremony performed at the Metropolitan Community Church in February 1978 after signing an agreement specifying that Richardson would perform the duties of a "wife" while Conley would provide financial support. Conley agreed in court to the support agreement.

**palimony suit, the most publicized lesbian**

Marilyn Barnett's against tennis pro Billie Jean King, filed in April 1981. The former Beverly Hills hairdresser who had served as secretary to King claimed that she and King had had a lesbian relationship for seven years and that she was therefore entitled to half of King's earnings from that time as well as King's Malibu beach house. At first dismissing Barnett's claims, King later acknowledged their relationship. In November 1982, the case was thrown out of court.

### parents, the first gay to adopt each other's kids

A lesbian couple in Washington, D.C. In a ruling announced July 26, 1991, Judge Geoffrey Alprin, head of the D.C. Superior Court's Family Division, granted the joint adoption that allowed the two women, who had been together for twelve years, to become legal coparents of their two children, one five, the other two. One woman had given birth to the older child after artificial insemination using an unknown donor's sperm. The other woman had adopted the younger child, who had been abandoned at birth in Nicaragua. The two children now use a hyphenated version of their mothers' last names.

### state, the first U.S. to decriminalize homosexuality

Illinois, repealing its sodomy laws in 1961. Effective January 1962, behavior between "consenting adults in private" was no longer subject to criminal prosecution.

### state, the first U.S. to pass a gay civil rights law

Wisconsin, on February 25, 1982. The legislature passed the bill after extensive efforts by Representative David Clarenbach. Governor Lee S. Dreyfus, a Republican, signed the bill into law.

### state or province, the first in North America to pass a gay civil rights law

Quebec. The province passed a statute December 16, 1977, banning discrimination against gay individuals in employment, housing, and public accommodations.

# THE ARTS

## VISUAL

### art exhibit, New York's first lesbian

"A Lesbian Show," conceived and organized by Harmony Hammond, and shown at the 112 Workshop gallery in early 1978. Seventeen lesbian artists exhibited work ranging from the abstract to the political.

### art festival, the first national lesbian

The National Lesbian Art Festival, held September 1 to October 8, 1978, at San Francisco's Gay Community Center. More than seventy-five artists from across the country showed their work. Events during the festival included theatre performances, live trapeze acts, and film screenings.

### arts center, the first gay in the U.S.

The Glines, founded in New York in April 1976. John Glines created the center as a "forum for playwrights, sculptors, actors, poets, choreographers, singers, directors, filmmakers, craftspeople, dancers, photographers, painters, musicians..." The Glines was also the first gay arts center to receive government funding, from the National Endowment for the Arts.

## LITERATURE

### anthology, the first true gay male

*Lieblingminne und Freundesliebe in der Weltliteratur* [*The Love of Comrades and Friends in World Literature*], compiled by Elisàr von Kupffer and published in Berlin in 1900.

### bibliography, the first annotated of lesbian literature

*Women Loving Women: A Select and Annotated Bibliography of Women Loving Women in Literature,* published by Woman-press in 1974. The 32-page pamphlet, with some 200 entries covering works published between 1914 and 1974, was published in conjunction with the first national lesbian writers' conference.

### bibliography, the first black lesbian

*Black Lesbians,* by J.R. Roberts (Barbara Rae Henry), published by Naiad in 1981. The annotated bibliography listed materials by and/or about black lesbians, from an ancient legend about black Amazons in what is now California, through the late 1970s.

### bibliography, the first English-language lesbian

*The Lesbian in Literature: A Bibliography,* compiled by Barbara Grier, under the pseudonym Gene Damon, and Lee Stuart in 1967. An outgrowth of the *Ladder,* the first edition included some three thousand books published through 1965. It had been preceded by two brief booklists compiled by Marion Zimmer Bradley in 1958 ("Astra's Tower Special Leaflets #2 and #3") and a hand-typed, mimeographed bibliography called "The Checklist" put out by Bradley and Grier in 1960.

### bibliography, the first gay-positive

*A Gay Bibliography,* published in January 1971. This list of 37 gay-positive books, pamphlets, and articles was compiled by Barbara Gittings of the American Library Association's Task Force on Gay Liberation (now the Gay and Lesbian Task Force). Updated four times over the next four years, by its sixth edition in 1980 it contained more than 600 entries.

**book, the best-selling gay male**

Patricia Nell Warren's *The Front Runner* (1974) or Armistead Maupin's *Tales of the City*. *Tales of the City* was first published in serial form, beginning with five episodes in Marin County's *Pacific Sun* in 1974, then in full in the *San Francisco Chronicle* starting May 24, 1976.

**book, the best-selling lesbian**

Rita Mae Brown's *Rubyfruit Jungle,* published by Daughters in 1973, or Radclyffe Hall's *The Well of Loneliness,* first published in 1928.

**book, the first gay**

The epic of Gilgamesh, composed in Sumerian in the third millenium B.C. In this homoerotic Mesopotamian epic poem, Gilgamesh, ruler of the Uruk people, is transformed by love for his comrade, Enkidu, into a virtuous ruler.

**book, the first homoerotic German**

*Ein Jahr in Arkadien [A Year in Arcadia]*, by Herzog August von Sachsen Gotha, published in 1805.

**book award, the first gay**

The American Library Association Task Force on Gay Liberation's (now GLTF) Gay Book Award. The first award, presented in 1971, went to Alma Routsong, alias Isabel Miller, for the self-published *A Place for Us,* which McGraw-Hill subsequently published as *Patience and Sarah.*

### book series, North America's first lesbian studies

The Cutting Edge: Lesbian Life and Literature. Published by
New York University Press and edited by longtime activist
Karla Jay, the series features previously out-of-print classics as
well as new literature, and encompasses new lesbian scholarship across a range of disciplines as well as nonacademic writing. The first six volumes of the series appeared in the summer
of 1992.

### bookstore, the first gay and lesbian (that was not an adult bookstore)

The Oscar Wilde Memorial Bookshop, opened by Craig Rodwell in New York City's Greenwich Village on Thanksgiving
Day, 1967. It claims to be the first gay bookshop in the world.

### bookstore, the first lesbian/feminist in the U.S.

The Amazon Bookstore in Minneapolis, Minnesota, founded in
1970, appears to have been the first, though A Woman's Place
was begun about the same time in Oakland, California. Two
women started Amazon out of their home. Run by volunteers
until the late 1970s and now an employee-owned for-profit
business, the store celebrated its twentieth anniversary in September 1990.

### bookstore, the largest feminist in the U.S., in annual volume

Women and Children First in Chicago, according to Judith
Rosen, writing for *Publishers Weekly*.

### bookstore, the largest gay and lesbian, in annual volume

Lambda Rising in Washington, D.C., has the highest annual dol-
lar volume of any gay and lesbian bookstore in the country.

**bookstore, the largest gay and lesbian, in annual volume for multiple stores**
A Different Light, with bookstores in New York, San Francisco, and West Hollywood.

**bookstore, the largest gay and lesbian, in number of titles**
Giovanni's Room in Philadelphia, with about 13,000 gay and lesbian titles. (The store also carries another 5,000 feminist books that are not specifically lesbian; these were not included in comparing it with other stores.)

**fiction writer, the first to incorporate the subject of AIDS in his work**
Armistead Maupin, in 1983, in his *Tales of the City* series in the *San Francisco Chronicle*.

**French Academy honorée, the first lesbian (and woman)**
Marguerite Yourcenar (1903–1987), inducted in 1981. From her first novel, *Alexis,* written in 1929, the chief subject of this French writer and intellectual was homosexual men, whom she rendered vitally and positively, primarily in historical fiction. Her lifelong companion was Grace Frick, an American with whom she lived for over forty years.

**guidebook, the first known gay**
*Granada: Guía emocional,* by Martínez Sierra, with photos by "Garzón" (literally, "an ephebe"), published in 1911. It was a guide to the Spanish city of Granada.

### Lambda Literary Award recipient, the first

Paul Monette, for *Borrowed Time*. The award, which was for Gay Men's Nonfiction, was presented by Sasha Alyson and, in Monette's absence, accepted by David Groff, at the First Annual Lambda Literary Awards ceremony, held June 2, 1989, in Washington, D.C.

### library, the first circulating lesbian in the U.S.

The New Alexandria Library of Lesbian/Wimmin, founded in Chicago in 1974 by J.R. Roberts. The only community lending library of its kind at the time, in 1975 it had over 1000 volumes in circulation. It was moved to Massachusetts some years later.

### Literary Guild selection, the first lesbian

*Patience and Sarah,* by Alma Routsong under the pseudonym Isabel Miller, in 1977.

### mail-order book service, the first gay

The Cory Book Service, founded by Donald Webster Cory (Edward Sagarin) in 1951 or 1952. The author of the ground-breaking 1951 book *The Homosexual in America* started the mail-order service to make publications on homosexuality more accessible to readers. Cory sold the service in early 1957 to a woman who renamed it the Winston Book Club. By 1967 the book club had some 5,000 members, but it died after being sold to two new owners in quick succession.

### manual, the first lesbian sex

*Loving Women,* written and published by the Nomadic Sisters collective in 1975.

**memoir, the first openly lesbian**

*A Narrative of the Life of Mrs. Charlotte Charke (Youngest Daughter of Colley Cibber, Esq.),* written in England in 1755. Charlotte Charke was a flamboyant transvestite actress. In her memoirs, she depicts, among other things, her relationship with her "wife," "Mrs. Brown."

**Nobel Prize winner, the first gay for literature**

Jacinto Benavente (1866–1954), in 1922. Though this Spanish dramatist focused primarily on the theme of love, he was unable to portray his own way of loving in his work. The first openly gay writer to win the same prize was the Australian novelist Patrick White, who won it in 1973.

**Nobel Prize winner, the first lesbian (and woman) for literature**

Selma Lagerlöf (1858–1940), in 1909. This Swedish novelist, poet, biographer, dramatist, and educator was a leading figure in the revival of romanticism in Swedish literature. Lagerlöf's diaries and a collection of letters, published in 1990, document her lifelong relationship with Sophie Elkan, another writer.

**novel, the first American to explicitly feature homosexuality**

*A Marriage below Zero,* written by Alfred J. Cohen under the pseudonym Chester Allan Dale and published in 1899. In it, Cohen uses a young woman narrator married to a homosexual man to promote his view that women should be warned about the disease of homosexuality to protect them from such marriages. This homophobic book established the tradition of having the main homosexual character commit suicide.

### novel, the first American to touch on gay themes

*Joseph and His Friend,* by the poet Bayard Taylor, published in 1870. Though the novel was dedicated "to those who believe in the truth and tenderness of man's love for man, as of man's love for woman," its homosexual elements were so subtle that a heterosexual reader could easily miss them.

### novel, the first gay-positive American

*Imre: A Memorandum,* written by Edward I. Prime-Stevenson under the pseudonym Xavier Mayne and published in 1908. In this novel, a man — the protagonist, Oswald — voluntarily admits his homosexuality — in this case, to Imre, the man he loves — for the first time in literary history. Imre eventually admits his own homosexuality and declares his equal, true love for Oswald.

### novel, the first lesbian by a woman

*Mary, a Fiction,* by Mary Wollstonecraft (1759–1797), published in 1788. Wollstonecraft based this novel on her real-life "consuming attachment" to Fanny Blood, a slightly older woman whom Wollstonecraft met when Fanny was fifteen, and loved until Fanny's death twelve years later.

### novel, the first sympathetic to man-boy love

*Fenny Skaller,* written in 1913 by the German writer and anarchist John Henry Mackay under the pseudonym Sagitta.

**novelist, the first major to make homosexuality a central theme**

Marcel Proust (1871–1922). The French writer featured many homosexual characters — major and minor — in his monumental semiautobiographical novel *A la recherche du temps perdu* [*Remembrance of Things Past*], published in sixteen volumes between 1913 and 1927. He also devoted much attention to lesbianism. His treatment of the subject of homosexuality did much to bring it into the mainstream of modern literature.

**press, the oldest surviving gay book in the U.S.**

Gay Sunshine Press in San Francisco. Founded in 1970 as a magazine publisher (it published the *Gay Sunshine Journal* through 1982), the press began publishing books in 1975.

**press, the oldest surviving lesbian in the U.S.**

Naiad Press, founded in 1973 by Barbara Grier in Tallahassee, Florida.

**science fiction story, the first gay**

*True History,* by the Greek writer Lucian (ca. A.D. 120–ca. 185). In this ironically titled work, the narrator travels to the moon, where he finds an all-male society that reproduces by giving birth from the thigh or by growing a child from a plant produced by planting the left testicle in the ground. After distinguishing himself in battle on behalf of the moon dwellers, the narrator is given the king's son in marriage.

### science fiction story, the first lesbian by a lesbian

An anonymously written story called "Kiki," published in *Vice Versa* in December 1947 appears to be the first, though a few stories with supernatural themes preceded it. In it, a supernatural entity called the Cosmic Registrar observes and records a "kiki" lesbian's search for true love.

### science fiction story, the first gay-positive

"The World Well Lost," by Theodore Sturgeon, published in the June 1953 issue of *Universe*. Two exiled androgynous, homosexual aliens arrive on Earth. Though initially fawning over the pair, when people discover the aliens' gender, they send them home to face execution. In the end, however, a closeted spaceman comes to their rescue.

### short story, the first gay by a black writer

"Smoke, Lilies and Jade," by Bruce Nugent. First published in 1926 in the controversial and short-lived *Fire!!,* it was reprinted in 1983 in the controversial gay anthology *Black Men/White Men.*

### writer, the first known lesbian

Sappho (ca. 612–ca. 560 B.C.). This classical Greek poet, proclaimed the "tenth Muse" for her lyricism, ran a school for the daughters of aristocrats on the island of Lesbos. The lyric poems she wrote celebrating her love for her pupils are the earliest known lesbian writings. Only about a twentieth of her work survives, in fragmentary form, after ecclesiastical authorities in Constantinople and Rome burned all known copies of her poems in 1073.

### writers' conference, the first national lesbian
Held in Chicago September 13–15, 1974, the first in a series of five. Some 100 to 150 women attended. Novelist Valerie Taylor was the keynote speaker. The conference was sponsored by Womanpress, a small lesbian press in Chicago.

### writers' fund, the first for emerging lesbian writers
The Lesbian Writers' Fund, established in 1990 by the Astraea National Lesbian Action Foundation. Each year, it awards $11,000 to each of five new lesbian writers — three fiction writers and two poets.

## THEATRE

### musical, the first openly gay
*The Faggot,* created by the Reverend Al Carmines in 1973.

### play, the first about AIDS
*One,* by Jeffrey Hagedorn. This one-man, one-act play premiered in Chicago in August 1983 with Carl Forsberg in the single role.

### play, the first about bisexuals
*Design for Living,* by Noel Coward. Most critics failed to recognize that the two men in the ménage à trois portrayed in this 1933 Broadway hit were lovers, however. Coward wrote the comedy, which he dedicated to drama critic Alexander Woollcott, so that he could costar in it with his close friends Alfred Lunt and Lynn Fontanne.

### play, the first by an American about a lesbian

*Sin of Sins,* by William Hurlbut. Isobel Elsom played the lesbian who kills the male sweetheart of the woman she loves, and seduces, in the 1926 production of this never-published play.

### play, the first by an American with a gay male character

*At Saint Judas's.* This one-act drama by Henry Blake Fuller was published in 1896 but never produced.

### play, the first English-language gay

*Edward II,* written by Christopher Marlowe in 1591 and first performed in 1593. Based on fact, Marlowe's play tells the story of the fourteenth-century English king who attempted to share his throne with his male lover, Gaveston. After thrice being exiled, Gaveston was finally hunted down and beheaded. Edward II himself was later forced to abdicate and murdered, reportedly by having a hot poker inserted into his anus. Marlowe's portrayal of the doomed relationship between the two men is sensitive and complex. The play was not professionally produced in the United States until 1958.

**play, the first English-language to portray lesbian characters**
*The God of Vengeance,* by Sholom Asch, translated from the
Yiddish *Gott fun Nekoma.* It was produced in 1922 by an
American woman, Alice Kauser, first at the Provincetown
Theater in Greenwich Village and then on Broadway. In *The
God of Vengeance,* the proprietor of a Jewish brothel buys a
Torah scroll to protect his teenage daughter, Rivkele, from the
sensuality of the brothel he runs in the cellar of their home.
Rather than being seduced by a male patron, however, Rivkele
becomes involved with one of the prostitutes, Manke, who
sneaks upstairs to visit the daughter and later proceeds to
seduce the young girl on stage in a frank and sensual scene.
The lovers were played by two little-known actors, Dorothee
Nolan and Virgina MacFayden, in the 1922 production.

**play, the first English-language to reward a homosexual
character**
*Whiteoaks,* by Mazo de La Roache, which opened on Broadway March 23, 1938. Finch is an effeminate, closeted musician
who is persecuted for his affections by his brothers. Nonethe-
less, by play's end, Finch stands to inherit his grandmother's
great fortune over her other relatives. "I know you're a queer
boy," his grandmother tells him, "but I like you — yes, I like
you very much." Ethyl Barrymore played the grandmother.

**play, the first gay-positive English-language**
*The Good,* by Chester Erskin. Though the play flopped, closing
after just nine performances at the Windsor Theatre in 1938, it
presented the subject of love between two men explicitly and
sympathetically. It was the first English-language play to
present a gay character without shame or guilt.

### play, the first to pit a liberated gay against a closeted one

*The Immoralist,* adapted by Ruth Goetz and Augustus Goetz from André Gide's novel in 1954. In the Goetzes' free adaptation, Michel, a refined, closeted, platonically married archeologist, is pitted against a free-thinking, educated Arab who has chosen a life in which he does not have to lie over professional success. Louis Jordan played Michel in the 1954 production; Geraldine Page played his wife, and a young, unknown James Dean played their Arab houseboy.

### play, the first with gay male characters on an American stage

*The Drag* (1927), written and produced by Mae West. Despite a successful tryout in Bridgeport, Connecticut, and a short run in New Jersey, *The Drag* never made it to Broadway: it was closed after West was jailed, in an unsuccessful attempt to censor her, for appearing in her first Broadway hit, *Sex. The Drag* included a highly theatrical scene of a wild drag party that was criticized as "glorifying" homosexuals; in truth, however, West had intended the play to call attention to a condition she considered a "disease."

### playwright, the first black lesbian (and woman) to have a play on Broadway

Lorraine Hansberry (1930–1965), in 1958. The play was *A Raisin in the Sun,* which won the New York Drama Critics' Circle Award.

### theatre group, the first gay

The Theater des Eros. Devoted exclusively to gay plays, this amateur theatre group, founded in Berlin in 1921, performed outspoken homosexual liberation plays in private homes from 1921 to 1924.

# FILM

### actor, the first to portray Jackie Kennedy on the screen

Divine, in John Waters's 1966 movie *Eat Your Makeup*. The low-budget, black-and-white 16mm film is about a mad governess who kidnaps models and makes them eat makeup and model themselves to death. Divine plays a thug who at one point imagines himself as Mrs. Kennedy during J.F.K.'s assassination. Howard Gruber played J.F.K. in the scene. According to Waters, "We didn't care who killed Kennedy. The point to us [in shooting the scene] was how great Jackie looked through it."

### character, the first lesbian in film

The Countess Geschwitz, played by the Belgian actress Alice Roberts, in the film *Pandora's Box* (*Die Büchse der Pandora*). G.W. Pabst directed the film, which starred Louise Brooks as Lulu, a woman "driven by insatiable lusts," in 1929. In the film, the countess is a passionate and somewhat self-sacrificing admirer of Lulu. The character was deleted from the British version of the film, but was restored sometime after its initial release in the United States. The film was based on a play by Frank Wedekind.

### film, the first gay

*Wingarne* [*Wings*]. Made in 1916 by Mauritz Stiller, the Swedish film was an early adaptation of a Danish novel by Hermann Bang, *Mikaël*, the story of a famous sculptor in love with a young man.

**film, the first gay rights**
> *Anders als die Andern* [*Different from the Others*], made by the Scientific-Humanitarian Committee in Berlin in 1919. The Committee managed to show it throughout most of Germany before the film was banned. This represented the first effort to use the medium of film to promote homosexual rights.

**film, the first to use the word *homosexual* on screen**
> *Victim,* in 1961. Dirk Bogarde starred as a gay lawyer who confronts a gang of blackmailers.

**film festival, the first (nonpornographic) gay male**
> Los Angeles, July 1968.

# MUSIC

**album, the first explicitly "in support of gays and lesbians" to feature major recording stars**
> *Get Out,* a CD anthology offered as a bonus to subscribers to the New York–based gay magazine *Out,* which debuted in June 1992. Included on the album were cuts from such artists as Deborah Harry, Lou Reed, k.d. lang, David Byrne, Morrisey, and Erasure.

**album, the first internationally distributed lesbian-produced lesbian**
> Alix Dobkin's *Lavender Jane Loves Women.* Dobkin produced the album with Kay Gardner and Marilyn Ries in New York in 1973.

**chorus, the first American gay**
The San Francisco Gay Men's Chorus, founded in early 1979.

**concert tour, the first European lesbian**
Alix Dobkin and a German duo known as Witch, consisting of Monika Jaeckel and Barbara Bauermeister, in 1979. The six-week tour covered Denmark, the Netherlands, Germany, Switzerland, Italy, and England.

**music festival, the first women's**
The first Michigan Womyn's Music Festival, held on 120 acres of open farmland in 1976. Some 2,000 women attended the three-day event. Performers included Maxine Feldman, Linda Tillery, and Holly Near.

**musical group, the first openly gay to play Carnegie Hall**
The New York City Gay Men's Chorus. They performed a Christmas concert December 8, 1981.

**musicians, the first openly lesbian to play Carnegie Hall**
Cris Williamson and Meg Christian, on November 26, 1982, in two standing-room-only concerts celebrating Olivia Records' tenth anniversary.

### performer, the first to come out on a record

Charles "Valentine" Harris, in January 1975, on the disco single "I Was Born This Way." The record, produced by Gaiee Records, became a number-one disco hit in London. But when Motown acquired the single and did little to promote it, it died. "I'm walking through life in nature's disguise / You laugh at me and you criticize / Just because I'm happy / I'm carefree / And I'm gay / Yes I'm gay / Tain't a fault 'tis a fact / I was born this way," went the lyrics, which were written by the woman president of Gaiee Records, Bunny Jones.

### rap record, the first gay

"Gay-Type Thang," by Jon Sugar. Fusion Records, a gay dance label, recorded the single in 1984, though the record was not actually pressed and released until June 1988.

### record, the best-selling lesbian of all time

Cris Williamson's *The Changer and the Changed*. Since it was cut in 1974 by Olivia Records, a quarter of a million copies have been sold.

### record, the first lesbian

A 45-rpm single of Lisa Ben singing her own "Cruisin' Down the Boulevard" and a lesbian version of "Frankie and Johnnie," recorded in the 1960s, appears to have been the first. The Los Angeles chapter of the Daughters of Bilitis produced the record on their own label as a fund-raising item, advertising it in issues of the *Ladder*. Often cited as the first is Maxine Feldman's 1972 "Angry Atthis" and "Amazon, " a 45-rpm single produced by Robin Tyler. Neither of these candidates, of course, takes into account the countless "race records" recorded in the 1920s and '30s by black artists such as Bessie Smith, Ma Rainey, Bessie Jackson, and others, many of which had lesbian lyrics. Two well-known examples are Ma Rainey's "Prove It on Me Blues" and Bessie Jackson's "B.D. Woman's Blues."

### record label, the first lesbian

Olivia Records, founded in Washington, D.C., in 1973 by a five-woman collective consisting of Ginny Berson, Judy Dlugacz, Meg Christian, Kate Winter, and Helaine Harris. The company cut its first record in early 1974, a 45-rpm single featuring Meg Christian's "Lady" on one side and Cris Williamson's "If It Weren't for the Music" on the other.

### song, the first commercially successful political gay

"Glad to Be Gay," by Tom Robinson. Released in 1978, the punk rock song, which includes an angry cataloging of British homophobic practices, became an underground hit.

**song, the most famous written by a lesbian**

"America the Beautiful." Katharine Lee Bates (1859–1929), a professor at Wellesley College from 1885 to 1925, wrote this song in 1893, inspired by a trip cross-country (her first) to guest lecture at Colorado College. She was lovers with another Wellesley professor, Katharine Coman, for twenty-five years.

# THE MEDIA

# PRINT

### comic book, the first full-format, nationally distributed lesbian

*Dynamite Damsels,* written, illustrated, published, and distributed by Roberta Gregory in 1976.

### comic-book superhero, the first openly gay

Northstar. Half-human and half-elf, and able to move at the speed of light, Northstar first appeared in 1980 in the Marvel line of comic books as a member of a Canadian superhero team known as Alpha Flight. He was conceived by creator John Byrne as gay from the beginning, though his gayness was only gradually revealed. He explicitly came out in the March 1992 issue of *Alpha Flight,* declaring, "It is past time that people started talking about AIDS. About its victims. Those who die ... and those of us left behind."

### comic-strip character, the first to die of AIDS

Andy Lippincott of *Doonesbury,* on May 24, 1990. Cartoonist Garry Trudeau introduced the gay character, a law student who evolved into an attorney and political aide, on February 10, 1976. When he first came out, to a crestfallen Joanie Caucus, five newspapers refused to carry the sequence. He was diagnosed with AIDS in the strip in early 1989.

### mainstream magazine, the first with an openly gay top editor

The *New Republic.* This conservative, Washington-based opinion journal named 28-year-old Andrew Sullivan to its top editorial position in October 1991. Despite expectations by some that Sullivan's sexuality would discourage advertisers, the magazine has thrived. Sullivan is also British and a Roman Catholic.

### newspaper, the first daily to publish same-sex domestic-partnership notices

*Everett* (Washington) *Herald*. In December 1990, this local daily became the first in the country to publish such notices when it ran a wedding announcement from Everett residents Sally Hutson and Jennifer Quall. The *Marin* (California) *Independent Journal* and the *Brattleboro* (Vermont) *Reformer*, both of which also have circulations under 75,000, quickly followed suit. On March 21, 1991, the *Minneapolis Star-Tribune*, which has a circulation of more than 400,000, became the first major daily to print partnership notices.

### newspaper, the first gay daily

The *Montrose Voice*, in Houston, Texas. The weekly gay paper tried in November 1986 to publish daily but found it did not have enough advertising to sustain the effort. It cut back to twice a week after just one week, and after six months went back to weekly publication.

### newspaper, the first to print a gay wedding announcement

*Mom ... Guess What!*, a Sacramento gay paper, first reported a gay wedding in 1978. It printed its first anniversary announcement in 1980.

### newspaper, the largest gay weekly in the U.S., in terms of circulation

The San Francisco-based *Bay Area Reporter*, with a circulation of 37,000. The BAR averages 64 to 72 pages per edition and may print 65,000 to 70,000 copies of special issues, such as the annual gay pride issue.

**newspaper columnist, the first to write about gay issues for a mainstream paper**

Deb Price. On May 8, 1992, Price became the first gay or lesbian columnist to write solely about gay topics for a mainstream daily metropolitan newspaper. Her column appears each Friday in the *Detroit News,* which has a readership of 450,000, as well as being offered to other Gannett papers nationwide.

**periodical, England's first national gay**

*Gay News.* The paper debuted June 27, 1972, and ceased publication April 14, 1983. During its run, editor Denis Lemon had the dubious distinction of being the first person in fifty-five years to be convicted of blasphemy, for printing a homoerotic poem about Christ written by James Kirkup. He was convicted July 12, 1977.

**periodical, the first American gay liberation**

*Friendship and Freedom.* Henry Gerber managed to publish two issues of this mimeographed newsletter in 1925 before being falsely arrested and losing his job.

**periodical, the first American lesbian**

*Vice Versa.* Under the pseudonym of Lisa Ben (an anagram of *lesbian*), a Los Angeles woman began publishing *Vice Versa: America's Gayest Magazine* in June 1947. Once a month for nine months she would type each issue manually, making five carbons for each original and circulating copies by having them passed from one reader to another.

**periodical, the first bisexual**

*Bisexual Liberation,* published by National Bisexual Liberation in the early 1970s.

### periodical, the first black gay

*Fire!!* A single issue published in 1926 showcased the best and brightest of the Harlem Renaissance, including work by Langston Hughes, Countee Cullen, Zora Neale Hurston, and Bruce Nugent. Highly controversial in the African-American community, it was meant to be a quarterly. Most copies of the magazine went up in flames when the building they were stored in burned, leaving the magazine's sponsors a thousand dollars in debt.

### periodical, the first black lesbian

*Onyx,* a bimonthly newsletter started in 1982 in Berkeley, California, by a black lesbian collective, appears to have been the first. A separate, San Francisco–based publication called the *Black Lesbian Newsletter* was publishing at about the same time.

### periodical, the first devoted to same-sex couples

*Partners Magazine for Gay and Lesbian Couples.* Begun as a newsletter in December 1986 by Stevie Bryant and Demian, it remains the only such publication to be supported by subscriptions. It is now a quarterly magazine.

### periodical, the first for blind gays and lesbians

*Lambda Resource Center for the Blind Quarterly.* This quarterly digest of selected English-language articles on gay history, culture, travel, personalities, books, music, entertainment, and general consciousness raising was published on cassette tapes. The first issue came out in July 1981; the last in April 1986, for a total of twenty issues. The Lambda Resource Center for the Blind was first organized in October 1979.

**periodical, the first known gay**

*Uranus.* Karl Heinrich Ulrichs began this German periodical for "Urnings" in 1870, after four years of planning. It died after a single issue for lack of support.

**periodical, the first known lesbian**

*Die Freundin* [*The Girlfriend*]. This German magazine, published in the late 1920s and early 1930s, openly discussed lesbian issues.

**periodical, the first known successful gay**

*Der Eigene: Ein Batt für mannliche Kultur* [*The Exceptional: A Magazine for Male Culture*]. Adolf Brand began publishing this German magazine in April 1896, editing it to its end, in 1931. When first begun, *Der Eigene* was subtitled *Monthly for Art and Life,* but in July 1899, after the Scientific-Humanitarian Committee was founded, the subtitle was changed to openly reflect the magazine's focus. The homoerotic literature and art that filled its pages reflected Brand's personal idealization of pederasty, as well as his interest in anarchism, theosophy, and nudism.

**periodical, the first national lesbian-feminist in the U.S.**

The *Furies.* Based in Washington, D.C., the *Furies* was founded in 1972 by a group of radical lesbians including Rita Mae Brown, Charlotte Bunch, Joan Biren, Sharon Deevey, Ginny Berson, and others. The collective published ten issues before disbanding in 1973.

**periodical, the first North American to use *gay* in its title**

*Gay* (later *Gay International*), founded in Toronto in 1964.

**periodical, the first scholarly gay**

*Jahrbuch für sexuelle Zwischenstufen* [*Yearbook for Sexual Intergrades*], founded in 1899 by the Scientific-Humanitarian Committee in Berlin and edited by Magnus Hirschfeld. This first journal of homosexual scholarship featured articles by experts in their fields covering all aspects of homosexuality, as well as reviews of fiction and nonfiction on the subject and commentary on relevant current events. Twenty-three volumes appeared in all. Publication ended in 1923, for financial reasons.

**periodical, the first scholarly gay in North America**

*ONE Institute Quarterly of Homophile Studies,* founded in 1968 after *ONE Magazine* ended. It ceased publication in 1973.

**periodical, the first wide-circulation gay in North America**

*ONE Magazine: The Homosexual Viewpoint.* Its first issue appeared in January 1953. By the mid-fifties there were thousands of each issue in circulation, with subscribers in every U.S. state, Europe, Asia, Australia, and South America. The monthly was the first gay magazine in the U.S. to reach a wide audience — 5,000 at its peak — though its publishers had to go to the Supreme Court to get the local postmaster to let them distribute it through the mail. *ONE* reported on entrapment and harassment cases, as well as publishing intellectual and cultural articles. It stopped regular publication in December 1969.

**periodical, the largest gay, in terms of circulation**

*Die Insel* [*The Island*]. According to scholars David Galloway and Christian Sabisch, this Berlin-based magazine boasted a circulation of 150,000 in 1930 — far more than any gay magazine currently publishing in the U.S.

**periodical, the largest gay in the U.S., in terms of circulation**

The *Advocate,* a biweekly with a circulation of 95,000 to 100,000 per issue.

**periodical, the largest lesbian in the U.S., in terms of circulation**

*Deneuve,* a San Francisco–based bimonthly glossy. Its circulation has rocketed since its first issue in May 1991 sold out its initial print run of 3,000. Owner and publisher Frances Stevens estimates *Deneuve*'s current circulation to be in the "high 30,000s," with a projected print run of 39,000 for the November 1992 issue.

**periodical, the oldest large-circulation gay in the U.S.**

The *Advocate.* Now a slick glossy, the magazine began in September 1967 as the mimeographed newsletter of PRIDE (Personal Rights in Defense and Education), a gay advocacy group. When PRIDE dissolved less than a year later, founder and editor Dick Michaels bought the magazine for $1. The first nationally distributed large-circulation gay periodical in the United States, the *Advocate* celebrated its twenty-fifth anniversary in its October 6, 1992, issue. ·

**periodical, the oldest large-circulation lesbian in the U.S.**

The *Lesbian Connection,* a bimonthly founded in East Lansing, Michigan, in August 1974 by the Ambitious Amazons collective. They currently print 20,000 to 21,000 copies per issue.

# RADIO

**radio program, the first lesbian-oriented African-American**
"Les Chanteuses Africaines," produced and hosted by Alicia
Banks. Broadcast Mondays, 1–4 a.m. on WRFG (89.3 FM) in
Atlanta since 1988, the show celebrates the musical and
literary voices of black women with an emphasis on lesbian
and feminist voices.

**radio program, the first to feature open homosexuals**
A show produced by Charles Hayden (a.k.a. Randolphe Wicker) in the summer of 1962. Aired on listener-supported WBAI
in New York, the program featured seven homosexuals talking
about their sexuality.

**radio talk show, the first commercial lesbian, gay, and
bisexual**
"Closet Free Radio," on WALE (990 AM) in Providence, Rhode
Island. The show premiered October 25, 1991, two weeks after
the original male cohost, Mike Connors, then a news anchor at
WALE, came out live on the air during a National Coming Out
Day show. Now cohosted by Cecilie Surasky and newcomer
Glenn Klein, the live, call-in talk show currently airs Monday
and Friday evenings, 6–8 p.m. It is still one of only a handful
of queer-oriented talk shows to be broadcast on commercial
radio. Other pioneers include "Hibernia Beach," broadcast at 7
a.m. Sunday mornings on KITS in San Francisco, and "The
Connie Norman Show," broadcast nightly on 95 AM in Los
Angeles.

# TELEVISION

### character, the first regular lesbian in a prime-time series

Nurse-practitioner Marilyn McGrath on ABC's "Heartbeat." The show was canceled in 1989 after a massive anti-gay letter-writing campaign initiated by CleaR-TV (Christian Leaders for Responsible Television) and AFA (American Family Association).

### character, the first regular transvestite on television

Corporal Max Klinger, on "M*A*S*H." Introduced in the CBS series' first season (1972–1973), the unequivocally heterosexual Corporal Klinger, played by Jamie Farr, wore outlandish women's outfits in a never-ending but futile attempt to get discharged from the army.

### characters, the first regular gay characters on television

Gordon and George, on "Hot L Baltimore," a short-lived 1975 sitcom produced by Norman Lear for ABC. The middle-aged couple, played by Henry Calvert and Lee Bergere, was among a cast of eccentric characters, all residents of a once-posh hotel. Also part of the cast were a latent lesbian named Jackie, played by Robin Wilson, and a South American prostitute. The show debuted January 24, 1975, and lasted just five months.

### characters, the first regular openly gay black on television

Blaine and Antoine, on Fox's "In Living Color." The two culture critics first appeared in 1990.

### game show host, the first lesbian

Hella von Sinnen, cohost of the German game show "Alles, Nichts, Oder!?" ["All, Nothing, Or!?"]. Von Sinnen came out in 1990 while accepting a Bambi — the German equivalent of an Emmy — for her work on "Alles, Nichts, Oder!?" "I would like to thank my wife for her support," she said, sparking a national media storm.

### kiss, the first full-fledged between two women on a network television series

Between Abby (Abigail Perkins, played by Michele Greene) and C.J. Lamb (played by Amanda Donohoe), on NBC's "L.A. Law." The episode aired February 7, 1991. Afterward, Abby assured C.J., "I like men," while C.J. revealed she was "flexible."

### performer, the first openly gay on network television

Terry Sweeney. He joined the cast of "Saturday Night Live" on November 9, 1985. His impersonations of First Lady Nancy Reagan quickly gained national attention.

### person, the first to actually come out on national television

Lance Loud, on PBS's "An American Family." The twelve-episode documentary series, which premiered January 15, 1973, followed an "average American family" — the Louds of Santa Barbara, California — for seven months, with the film crew essentially living with the family from May 1971 to the following New Year's Eve. During the course of the filming, eighteen-year-old Lance declared himself "Homo of the Year."

### soap opera, the first lesbian

"Two in Twenty," produced by Laurel Chiten on videotape.
The series premiered in January 1988 in Somerville, Massachusetts, to a sold-out theatre audience. More than 200 volunteers worked for over three years on the project. Five episodes were filmed in all. Available on videotape from Wolf Video in New Almaden, California, the series has been broadcast on local cable channels and screened in film festivals in cities all over the world.

### soap opera, the first to deal with teen homosexuality

ABC's "One Life to Live." On June 18, 1992, a male high school student, Billy Douglas, told his best friend, Joey Buchanan, that he is gay. Though initially shocked, Joey has worked hard to understand his friend, and their friendship has grown stronger. The daytime series has used the character to explore many gay issues, including homophobia and coming out to parents.

### soap opera, the first to feature the Quilt

ABC's "One Life to Live." The Quilt came to Llanview in August 1992.

### television actor, the first openly HIV-positive gay

Michael Kearns. Kearns guest-starred on the March 15, 1992, "Hearts and Flowers" episode of ABC's "Life Goes On." In the episode, Jesse, an HIV-positive high school student played by regular Chad Lowe, meets Kearns's character while volunteering at an AIDS hospice. "Lowe's character is the most responsible depiction of HIV on television," said Kearns, "because it isn't just one story about someone getting the disease and dying in the end. Here we see someone living with HIV, not dying from AIDS."

**television appearance, the first by a gay spokesperson on a major national network program**

On ABC's "Dick Cavett Show," November 27, 1970. Two spokesmen for the Gay Activists Alliance were guests: members Marty Robinson and Arthur Evans. The producers of the late-night talk show agreed to the appearance after learning that the GAA planned to disrupt the show in October "to draw attention to the vicious anti-gay remarks that have been said both by Mr. Cavett and by guests he has had on the show." Previously, the Reverend Troy Perry, pastor of MCC in LA, had appeared on two syndicated national shows, "The Virginia Graham Show" and "The Phil Donahue Show."

**television appearance, the first by an openly gay person**

One of the earliest appears to have been by Terry, the president of the Los Angeles chapter of DOB, who was interviewed on camera by Paul Coates at the time of the second DOB convention in 1962. Because Terry was self-employed, she could do so without fear of losing her job.

**television commercial, the first gay-oriented in the world**
Produced by Washington, D.C.'s Lambda Rising bookstore, the commercial aired four times on the local NBC and ABC affiliates (channels 4 and 7) in February 1975. The commercial featured images of various gays and lesbians wearing the lambda symbol as a voice-over explained the significance of the symbol, described the difficulty of obtaining gay and lesbian literature in mainstream bookstores, and told about the "bookstore that celebrates the gay and lesbian experience." Both stations initially balked at airing the commercial, but the industry watchdog at the time, the National Association of Broadcasters Standards Office, approved it. Channel 4 ran the commercial uncut; Channel 7 insisted that one "suggestion of nudity," an image of a shirtless man, be cut. The commercials aired during two different shows that dealt with gay themes, and generated much excitement but only a modicum of business.

**television commercial, the first national for condoms**
Fox Broadcasting Company aired a 15-second, AIDS-related pitch by Trojan in November 1991 during the sitcom "Herman's Head."

**television movie, the first nonhomophobic to focus on homosexuality**
*That Certain Summer,* broadcast by ABC on November 1, 1972. Hal Holbrook played a divorced gay father whose fourteen-year-old son learns about his homosexuality; Martin Sheen played his lover. *That Certain Summer* was written and produced by William Link and Richard Levinson. Scott Jacoby won an Emmy for Best Supporting Actor for his portrayal of the son.

### television movie, the first to deal with AIDS

*An Early Frost.* This Emmy-winning film, broadcast by NBC on November 11, 1985, starred Aidan Quinn as a young lawyer who must tell his family not only that he is gay but that he has AIDS.

### television series, the first dramatic in prime time to feature a regular gay character

ABC's "Dynasty." The series introduced Steven Carrington as the homosexual son of an oil tycoon in 1981, then copped out after one season: the father murdered the son's lover, and Carrington came to terms, at least temporarily, with his latent heterosexuality. Al Corley, the actor who originally portrayed Steven, quit, saying, "They had a chance to do something different and they chickened out." The character vacillated for the rest of the series' run, but was "definitely" gay when the series ended in 1989.

### television series, the first in prime time to deal with the topic of AIDS

CBS's "Trapper John, M.D." An episode broadcast in November 1985 was the first show on television to address this issue. A week later, NBC broadcast *An Early Frost,* which won three Emmys and is credited with breaking the taboo on AIDS.

### television series, the first nationally produced American gay and lesbian

"In the Life." A preview of the hour-long variety show aired on Public Broadcasting stations nationwide in June 1992. Coproduced by PBS affiliate WNYC in New York and John Scagliotti, producer of the documentary film *Before Stonewall,* the monthly show was scheduled to begin its regular broadcast in New York, San Francisco, and other markets in the fall of 1992.

**television series, the first network to show two gay men in bed together**
ABC's "thirtysomething." On November 7, 1989, Russell Weller (played by semiregular David Marshall Grant) and Peter Montefiore appeared in bed together, talking, apparently naked, enjoying a postcoital afterglow — without touching. The scene aroused so much controversy that ABC reportedly lost $1.5 million in canceled advertising when five of the show's ten sponsors pulled ads.

**television show, the first network to show gay characters**
"N.Y.P.D." Its first episode, "The Shakedown," which aired September 5, 1967, focused on a blackmail ring that preyed on gay people. The show included an empathetic black policeman who showed strong support for the gay characters. This marked the first time the word homosexual had been used in any network drama.

**television show, the first to focus on homosexuality**
David Susskind's "Open End," in the late 1950s. The therapists who appeared as his guests agreed that homosexuals were sick people.

**television special, the first on homosexuality**
"The Rejected." Aired in 1963 by station KQED in San Francisco, the show featured Margaret Mead among its guests.

**television station, the first to run condom ads**
KRON in San Francisco. On January 14, 1987, KRON became the first television station in the U.S. to run a condom ad. Not until November 1991 would such an ad air nationally.

# INDEX

## A

adoption, 84
*Advocate*, 115
Ai, 13
AIDS, 22, 31, 35, 42, 46, 74, 91, 97
"Alles, Nichts, Oder!?," 118
Amazon Bookstore, 90
"An American Family," 118
American Library Association, 43, 88–89
American Sociological Association, 44
"America the Beautiful," 106
Amsel, Robert, 79
Amsterdam, 16, 46
*Anders als die Andern.* See *Different from the Others.*
"Angry Atthis," 105
Ann Arbor (Michigan), 66, 68, 78
Antinoopolis, 12
Aristotle, 28
*Art of Love, The*, 11
Asch, Sholom, 99
Astraea National Lesbian Action Foundation, 36, 97
*At Saint Judas's*, 98
Atlas Savings and Loan, 35

## B

Baker, Gilbert, 36
Baker, Jack, 56, 81
Bancroft, Ann, 40
Bang, Hermann, 101
Banks, Alicia, 116
Barnett, Marilyn, 83
Barrett, Ellen Marie, 60
Bates, Katharine Lee, 106
*Bay Area Reporter*, 110
Belew, Judith Ann, 79–80
Ben, Lisa, 105, 111
ben-Shalom, Miriam, 82
Benavente, Jacinto, 93
Benedict IX, 19
Bennett, Allen, 60

Bennett, Michael, 35
Berkeley (California), 77
Beth Chayim Chadashim, 61
Beth Simchat Torah, 62
Bird, Merton, 44
*Bisexual Liberation*, 43, 111
*Black Lesbian Newsletter*, 112
*Black Lesbians*, 88
book club, 92
Booker, Bob, 38
Boozer, Melvin, 65
Boston Asian Gay Men and Lesbians, 43
Boston Fire Department, 35
Bradley, Marion Zimmer, 88
Brand, Adolf, 17, 113
Bronx High School of Science, 54
Brown, Dr. Howard, 47
Brown, Jerry, 69–70
Brown, Rita Mae, 89
Buchanan, James, 22
*bull-dyke*, 25
Bush, George, 72
Byton High School, 54

## C

Campbell, Bobbi, 48
Carmines, Al, 97
Carter, Jimmy, 73
Casper, Johann Ludwig, 26
Chaddock, Charles, 22, 24
*Changer and the Changed, The*, 104
Charke, Charlotte, 93
Chasnoff, Debra, 46
child custody, 79, 82
Chizh, Vladimir Fiodorovich, 27
Christian, Meg, 103, 105
Church of ONE Brotherhood, 59
Churchill, Wainwright, 23
Clinton, Bill, 66
"Closet Free Radio," 116
COC, 46
Cohen, Alfred, 93

Committee of Friends on Bisexuality, 60
Connors, Mike, 116
Cordova, Jeanne, 40
Cornish, Richard, 12
Cory Book Service, 92
Cory, Donald Webster, 92
Costanza, Midge, 73
Council on Religion and the Homosexual, 61
Coward, Noel, 97
Cox, Rudi, 39
Crete, 15
"Cruisin' Down the Boulevard," 105
cruising, 11
Cutting Edge, 90

## D

Dale, Chester Allan. See Cohen, Alfred.
Dallas Gay Alliance Credit Union, 34
Daly, James, 82
Damon, Gene. See Grier, Barbara.
Daughters of Bilitis, 33, 44, 105, 120
Davis, Madeline, 67
death penalty, 13, 16, 79
Deaton, Charles, 34
DeGrieck, Gerald, 68
Delta Lambda Phi, 53
Democratic National Convention: 1972, 67; 1980, 65; 1988, 48; 1992, 66
*Deneuve*, 115
Denmark, 21, 78, 81
*Der Eigene*, 113
*Design for Living*, 97
*Detroit News*, 111
"Dick Cavett Show," 120
*Die Freundin*, 113
*Die Insel*, 114
*Different from the Others*, 102
A Different Light, 91
Dignity, 61
Dillon, Michael, 20

District of Columbia City Council, 79
Divine, 101
Dobkin, Alix, 102–103
domestic partnership, 77
Donaldson, Stephen, 39, 55, 60
Dong Xian, 13
*Doonesbury*, 109
*Drag, The*, 100
*Duan xiu pian.* See *Records of the Cut Sleeve.*
dyke, 25
*Dynamite Damsels*, 109
"Dynasty," 122

**E**

*Early Frost, An*, 122
East Coast Homophile Organizations, 33, 68
East Lansing (Michigan), 77
Eastern Regional Conference of Homophile Organizations, 33, 41
*Eat Your Makeup*, 101
Ebersole, Robert, 69
ECHO. See East Coast Homophile Organizations.
*Edward II*, 98
Ellis, Havelock, 25
*Encyclopedia of Sexual Knowledge, The*, 13
entrapment, 32, 36
ERCHO. See Eastern Regional Conference of Homophile Organizations.
*Eros: The Male Love of the Greeks*, 11, 16, 20
Ersine, Noel, 23
Erskin, Chester, 99
Eulenburg, Philipp von, 17, 21, 24
Evans, Arthur, 120
*Everett* (Washington) *Herald*, 110

**F**

*Faggot, The*, 97
Feldman, Marvin, 46

Feldman, Maxine, 105
*Fenny Skaller*, 94
*Fire!!*, 96, 112
Foster, George, 38
Foster, Jim, 67
Frank, Barney, 68
"Frankie and Johnnie," 105
Fricke, Aaron, 55
*Friendship and Freedom*, 43, 111
*Front Runner, The*, 89
Fuller, Henry Blake, 98
*Furies*, 113

**G**

Gann, Keith, 48
*Gay*, 113
Gay Activists Alliance, 15, 55, 120
Gay and Lesbian Community Services Center, 74
Gay and Lesbian Hall of Fame, 38
Gay and Lesbian History on Stamps Club, 49
Gay and Lesbian Task Force, 72. See Task Force on Gay Liberation.
*Gay Bibliography, A*, 88
Gay Bob, 35
Gay Community Services Center, 72
Gay Games, 37, 48
Gay Liberation Front, Tri-Cities, 49
Gay Men's Chorus: New York, 103; San Francisco, 103
*Gay News*, 111
gay pride, 41–42, 47, 49, 66
Gay Sunshine Press, 95
George Washington High School, 54
Gerber, Henry, 43, 111
Gernreich, Rudi, 45
*Get Out*, 102
Gide, André, 11, 100
Gilgamesh, 89
Giovanni's Room, 91
Gittings, Barbara, 88
"Glad to Be Gay," 105
*God of Vengeance, The*, 99

Goetz, Ruth and Augustus, 100
Goldman, Emma, 19
*Good, The*, 99
Granada (Spain), 91
Greek vase paintings, 15
Gregory, Roberta, 109
Grier, Barbara, 88, 95

**H**

Hadrian, 12
Hagedorn, Jeffrey, 97
Haire, Norman, 13
Hall, Radclyffe, 89
Hamilton, Alexander, 22, 48
Hammon, Mary Vincent, 12
Hammond, Harmony, 87
Hansberry, Lorraine, 100
Harlem Renaissance, 112
Harris, Charles, 104
Harris, Sherry, 69
Hate Crimes Statistics Act, 72
Hatshepsut, 12
Hay, Harry, 45
Hayden, Charles. See Wicker, Randy.
"Heartbeat," 117
Heckman, Neva, 79–80
Hein, Marc, 48
Heliogabalus, 21
Hennefeld, Paul, 49
Hiller, Kurt, 28
*Hippocratic Corpus*, 28
Hirschfeld, Magnus, 17, 114
Hitchens, Donna, 70
Hoessli, Heinrich, 11, 16, 20
Holocaust, 16, 18
Homo-Monument, 16
*Homosexual Behavior among Males*, 23
Homosexual Information Center, 72
Homosexual League of New York, 67
Hooker, Evelyn, 27
Horton, Lester, 36
Hotel Employees and Restaurant Employees Union, San Francisco, 74
"Hot L Baltimore," 117
Hull, Bob, 45

Human Rights Campaign Fund, 72
Hurlbut, William, 98
Hutson, Sally, 110

**I**

"I Was Born This Way," 104
*If It Die*, 11
Illinois, 84
*Immoralist, The*, 100
*Imre: A Memorandum*, 94
"In Living Color," 117
"In the Life," 122
International Gay and Lesbian Archive, 31

**J**

*Jahrbuch für sexuelle Zwischenstufen*, 114
Jay, Karla, 90
Jennings, Dale, 32, 36, 45
John XII, 19
Johnson, William, 60
Jones, Cleve, 42, 46
Jones, Randal, 82
Jorgensen, Christine, 21
*Joseph and His Friend*, 94

**K**

Kameny, Frank, 65, 68
Kearns, Michael, 119
Kennedy, Jackie, 101
Kepner, Jim, 31, 45
Kertbeny, Károly Mária, 24
"Kiki," 96
King, Billie Jean, 83
Klein, Don, 34
Kleist, Heinrich von, 21
Knights of the Clock, 44
Kopay, David, 31
Kozachenko, Kathy, 68
KQED, 123
Kreps, Denise, 39
KRON, 123
Kupffer, Elisàr von, 87

**L**

"L.A. Law," 118
La Roache, Mazo de, 99

Labonté, Richard, 37
Lachs, Stephen, 69
*Ladder*, 44, 88
Lagerlöf, Selma, 47, 93
Laius, 14
Lambda Delta Lambda, 56
Lambda Literary Awards, 92
*Lambda Resource Center for the Blind Quarterly*, 112
Lambda Rising bookstore, 90, 121
Laurens, John, 22, 48
*Lavender Jane Loves Women*, 102
Lavender U, 56
Lecomte, Raymond, 21
Legg, Dorr, 45
Leitsch, Dick, 79
Lemon, Denis, 111
"Les Chanteuses Africaines," 116
*Lesbian Connection*, 115
Lesbian Herstory Archives, 31
*Lesbian in Literature, The*, 88
"A Lesbian Show," 87
Lesbian Writers' Fund, 97
Leviticus, 16
*Lieblingminne und Freundesliebe in der Weltliteratur*. See *Love of Comrades and Friends in World Literature, The*.
"Life Goes On," 119
Lilly, Frank, 73
Lippincott, Andy, 109
Log Cabin Republican Club, 74
Lot, 14
*Love of Comrades and Friends in World Literature, The*, 87
Love, Barbara, 33
*Loving Women*, 92
Lucian, 95
Lyon, Phyllis, 33, 44

**M**

"M*A*S*H," 117
Mackay, John Henry, 94

*Magazine of Experimental Psychical Studies*, 26
March on Washington for Gay and Lesbian Rights: 1979, 41; 1987, 37, 50
"Marcus Welby, M.D.," 73
Marlowe, Christopher, 98
*Marriage below Zero, A*, 93
Martin, Del, 33, 44
Martin, Robert. See Donaldson, Stephen.
*Mary, a Fiction*, 94
Mattachine Society, 32, 36, 45
Maupin, Armistead, 89
Mayne, Xavier. See Prime-Stevenson, Edward.
McConnell, James Michael, 81
McIlvenna, Ted, 61
McKellen, Ian, 70
McWhirter, Martha, 20
Metropolitan Community Church, 59, 61, 80; Cathedral of Hope, 59
Michaels, Dick, 115
Michéa, Claude-François, 26
Michigan Womyn's Music Festival, 103
Milk, Harvey, 68
Miller, Isabel, 89, 92
*Minneapolis Star-Tribune*, 110
Mitchell, Camille, 82
*Molly*, 25
*Mom ... Guess What!*, 110
Monette, Paul, 92
*Montrose Voice*, 110
Morgan, Mary, 70
Murphy, Jim, 35

**N**

NACHO. See North American Conference of Homophile Organizations.
"N.Y.P.D.," 123
Naiad Press, 95
Names Project. See Quilt.
National Bisexual Liberation, 43, 111

National Coming Out Day, 42
National Gay Rights Advocates, 80
National Gay Task Force, 73
National Organization for Women, 33
National Planning Conference of Homophile Organizations. See North American Conference of Homophile Organizations.
New Alexandria Library of Lesbian/Wimmin, 92
*New Republic,* 109
Noble, Elaine, 69
Nomadic Sisters, 92
Norman, Sarah White, 12
North American Conference of Homophile Organizations, 32
Northstar, 109
Norway, 78
Nugent, Bruce, 96

**O**

Olivia Records, 34, 103–105
*One,* 97
ONE Institute, 54
*ONE Institute Quarterly of Homophile Studies,* 114
"One Life to Live," 119
*ONE Magazine,* 114
ONE, Inc., 45
*Onyx,* 112
"Open End," 123
Orpheus, 14
Oscar Wilde Memorial Bookshop, 90
*Out,* 102
Out of the Closet, Inc., 35
*Out of the Closets,* 38

**P**

Pacific Bell, 80
*Pandora's Box,* 101
Partners for AIDS-Free America, 38

*Partners Magazine for Gay and Lesbian Couples,* 112
*Patience and Sarah,* 89, 92
*People* magazine, 34
Pere-Lachaise Cemetery, 11
Perry, Troy, 80, 120
"Phil Donahue Show," 120
Phiops II, 12, 15
picket, 67–68
Pillard, Dr. Richard, 47
Pitzer College, 53
*Place for Us, A.* See *Patience and Sarah.*
Price, Deb, 111
PRIDE, 115
Pride Foundation of Seattle, 34
Prime-Stevenson, Edward, 94
Proust, Marcel, 95

**Q**

Quall, Jennifer, 110
Quebec, 80, 84
Quilt, the Names Project AIDS Memorial, 37, 42, 46

**R**

*Raisin in the Sun, A,* 100
Reagan, Ronald, 73
Reaugh, Ernest O., 40
*Records of the Cut Sleeve,* 14
"The Rejected," 123
*Remembrance of Things Past,* 95
Rimbaud, Arthur, 48
Roberts, J.R., 88, 92
Robigalia, 14
Robinson, Marty, 120
Robinson, Svend, 71
Robinson, Tom, 105
Rodwell, Craig, 90
Roff, Margaret, 70
Rohl, Randy, 55
ROTC, 53
Routsong, Alma. See Miller, Isabel.
Rowland, Chuck, 45
*Rubyfruit Jungle,* 89

**S**

Sachsen Gotha, Herzog August von, 89
Sacred Band of Thebes, 17
Sagitta, 94
San Francisco Police Department, 39
Sanctificationists, 20
Sappho, 96
Sarria, José, 65
"Saturday Night Live," 118
Scientific-Humanitarian Committee, 17–18, 102, 114
serpent, the, 14
*Sexual Inversion,* 25
Shocking Grey, 40
Short, James, 83
*Si le grain ne meurt.* See *If It Die.*
Sierra, Martínez, 91
*Sin of Sins,* 98
Slater, Don, 45
Smith, Chris, 71
"Smoke, Lilies and Jade," 96
Social Democratic party, 18
Society for Human Rights, 43
Society for Individual Rights, 33
Spear, Allan, 69
Springfield (Oregon), 78
St. John the Evangelist, 19
St. John, Keith, 68
Stuart, Lee, 88
Studds, Gerry, 68
Student Homophile League, 53, 55, 67
Sturgeon, Theodore, 96
Sullivan, Andrew, 109
Surasky, Cecilie, 116
Susskind, David, 123
Sweden, 47, 79
Sweeney, Terry, 118

**T**

*Tales of the City,* 89
Task Force on Gay Liberation, 43, 88–89
Taylor, Bayard, 94
Terrigno, Valerie, 71

*That Certain Summer*, 121
Theater des Eros, 100
"thirtysomething," 123
Timarchus, 19
Tomb of the Bulls, 15
Tomb of the Two
    Brothers, 13
Toronto (Canada), 81
"Trapper John, M.D.," 122
*True History*, 95
"Two in Twenty," 119
Tyler, Robin, 105

# U

Ulrich, Gerald, 70
Ulrichs, Karl Heinrich, 15,
    24, 113
*Underworld and Prison
    Slang*, 23
Unitarian Universalists, 59
*Uranus*, 113

# V

Vendola, Niki, 71
Verlaine, Paul, 48
*Vice Versa*, 96, 111
*Victim*, 102

Vilanch, Bruce, 38
Virginia Colony, 79
"Virginia Graham Show,"
    120
von Sinnen, Hella, 118

# W

Waddell, Tom, 34, 37
WALE, 116
Warren, Patricia Nell, 89
Washington, George, 22
Waters, John, 101
WBAI, 116
Wechsler, Nancy, 68
Weld, William, 69
*Well of Loneliness, The*, 89
West Hollywood (Califor-
    nia), 66
West, Mae, 100
Westphal, Karl Friedrich
    Otto, 26
White House, 33, 72
White, Patrick, 93
*Whiteoaks*, 99
Whitlock, Kay, 33
Wicker, Randy, 67, 116
Williamson, Cris, 103–105
*Wingarne*. See *Wings*.

*Wings*, 101
Wisconsin, 84
Wissenschaftlich-
    humanitäre Komitee.
    See Scientific-
    Humanitarian
    Committee.
Witch, 103
Wollstonecraft, Mary, 94
Womanpress, 88, 97
Women and Children First,
    90
*Women Loving Women*, 88
"The World Well Lost," 96
WRFG, 116
writers' conference, nation-
    al lesbian, 88

# Y

*Year in Arcadia, A*, 89
*Yearbook for Sexual Inter-
    grades*. See *Jahrbuch
    für sexuelle Zwis-
    chenstufen*.
Yourcenar, Marguerite, 91
Yuga-Duga, 41